THE CARITAS PATH TO PEACE

A Guidebook for Creating World Peace with Caring, Love, and Compassion

MARY ROCKWOOD LANE, PhD, RN, FAAN
MICHAEL SAMUELS, M.D
JEAN WATSON,
PhD, RN, AHN-BC, FAAN

DEDICATION PAGE

Mary Rockwood Lane

I would like to dedicate this book to my brother, Lawrence Peck Rockwood II, who speaks to the power of peace, truth, and justice.

Michael Samuels

I dedicate this book to the seven generations before and the seven generation after.

Jean Watson

I dedicate this part of my work to nurses all over the world and to my children, my grandchildren and all the children of the world who will have to carry this path and passage for new generations to come. Privately, I dedicate my work on caring and peace to D and R who both cracked opened my heart, inspired my soul and continue to help me to soar with my life work. They know who they are.

FOREWORD BY:

JEAN WATSON, PhD, RN, AHN-BC, FAAN

Distinguished Professor of Nursing

Murchinson-Scoville Endowed Chair in
Caring Science, University of Colorado
Denver

Founder & Chair of Board: Watson
Caring Science Institute www.
watsoncaringscience.org

jean@watsoncaringscience.org

The Caritas Path to Peace by Jean Watson, Mary Rockwood Lane, and Michael Samuels- A book endorsed by Watson Caring Science Institute

Foreword by Jean Watson, Author of Theory and Philosopher of Caring Science; Founder Watson Caring Science Institute

This Caritas Path to Peace shows us the way forward. It serves as a Waymarker on the path toward human caring and peace on earth. It is an inspired work which ushers in the collective evolution of humankind, toward a new consciousness, which unites and transcends time and space and previous ways of thinking about our life and relationship with our self, each other and Mother Earth. It heightens our awakening of the great change needed at this hour for sustaining humanity at this very point in human history.

Ancient wisdom from our ancestors, current wisdom from our enlightened leaders and wisdom seekers around the globe are proclaiming the time is now. The time is now, the hour is now for the great shift which we have been waiting for, moving us toward a moral community of caring and peace. We are reminded that we hold the vision to create a world free of war and violence; we as men, women, physicians, nurses and all health care workers and caretakers worldwide, are compassionate caregivers of creation of all of life; we hold visions of love and peace and miracles in our midst. We are here to serve and to co-create a new reality to protect and help reverse the fragility of our humanity and Planet Earth.

The Caritas Path to Peace helps us find our inner wisdom and our way forward as we become one with this great shift in human consciousness. This work is embedded in wisdom traditions and perennial knowledge from philosophers, theologians, wise elders and indigenous peoples on the Planet Earth and spirit world. This book is an invitation to hear the dreams of human kind, of Mother Earth so we all can heal; it is an invitation to participate in sustaining human caring in our world. It returns us to the heart and soul of our being and becoming as one great I AM for collective healing. The Caritas Path is a light in the darkness of emergence, now opening new horizons of beauty and love for all living things.

Mary and Michael draw upon diverse visions and wisdom leaders to show us the converging path to peace. In referencing Teilhard de Chardin , they quote: "No one can deny that a network (a world network) of economic and psychic affiliations is being woven at ever increasing speed which envelops and constantly penetrates more deeply within each of us. With every day that passes it becomes a little more impossible for us to act or think otherwise than collectively." Chardin believed that matter, and later life, is evolving towards knowledge of spirit. He believed the noosphere was like God seeing him or herself and was the emergence of pure conscious energy beyond the ego of one person acting alone for his own wishes. Chardin believed that this mega synthesis of the thinking elements of the earth towards a larger consciousness would result in a universal consciousness which would take us beyond war and greed.

This evolved consciousness captured by Chardin lives throughout this book and truly helps us find the Caritas Path to Peace which unites toward this knowledge and experience of Universal Love, the knowledge of Spirit which enfolds all.

My endorsement of this book is my Caritas Prayer for Peace. It is with the hope and faith that Watson Caring Science Institute and all men, women, physicians, nurses and health workers in the world help radiate this Caritas Path to Peace consciousness so it, and we, touch the heart of all who read it - touch the heart of our collective humanity, and at last touch the throbbing heart of Mother Earth who holds us in her embrace as we unite to "love all, serve all and heal the Planet".

Watson Caring
Science Institute

This is a personal global invitation to nurses and others to join this pilgrimage with Jean Watson as she travels around the globe.

As each one
of us walks in the
Spirit of Caring and Peace,
we are bringing in the
Light of Caritas Peace.

Everyday, we walk together from
wherever we are, holding this
energetic field and elevating higher
consciousness for healing.

WatsonCaringScience.org

We invite you to sign the Peace Proclamation on the WCSI web site. There is a page to sign your name, making you part of the Caritas Peace international community. This is a call to stand up and take your place in this world-wide Caritas Peace community.

You will bring your light to this work ~ the world has been waiting for you. Come stand in our circle as we all hold up this light for the reawakening of loving kindness, peace and caring on this precious planet. We need your light to make this work brighter for the ones in the darkness so they can find their way to live in peace.

 facebook.com/wcsi.cares   twitter.com/wcsi

INTERNATIONAL CHARTER IN HUMAN CARING (ICHC)
PROPOSED BY JEAN WATSON, Ph.D, RN, AHN-BC, FAAN
DISTINGUISHED PROFESSOR AND MURCHINSON-SCOVILLE ENDOWED CHAIR IN CARING SCIENCE
UNIVERSITY OF COLORADO DENVER, COLLEGE OF NURSING, FOUNDER & CHAIR OF THE BOARD:
WATSON CARING SCIENCE INSTITUTE
WatsonCaringScience.org

TO BE PRESENTED AT THE FIRST ASIAN –PACIFIC INTERNATIONAL CARITAS CONSORTIUM AND
INTERNATIONAL CARING AND PEACE CONFERENCE:
HIROSHIMA, JAPAN, MARCH 2012

PROLOGUE AND BASIC PREMISES
At this time in human history the survival of humanity and Earth Mother's eco-system is
threatened. Every human on earth shares and draws upon Earth Mother/Sky Father and
helps to evolve the Planet with caring for all. Each society sustains human caring and
humanity for the whole. The practices of human caring are practices of peace. In order to
sustain humanity and the Planet Earth, the following premises are proclaimed as a formal
Charter for Human Caring and Peace:

Every person in the world has the right to receive humane and compassionate care; • Every human on
earth shares and draws upon all the eco-system for survival; • Every human is here on the earth plane for
a reason and unique life-purpose; • All of humanity is joined in the infinite field of the universe with
each other and all living things; • All creation is sacred and connected; • Each person's level of
humanity reflects upon the whole, allowing for the collective growth of human consciousness for all
of humankind; • Globally, women and children and nurses in society, carry the predominance of
human caring for all of humanity, helping to sustain human caring and humanity for the whole;
• The human caring needs of women and children in the world are threatened; • All humans are
entitled to be free of tyranny, violation, abuse – free to pursue their dreams and follow their heart;
• All humans 'Belong' to Infinite Source, the sacred mystery, which unites ALL, before, during
and after the Planet Earth plane experience; • Finally. if we want to sustain human caring
and peace, begin first with personal self-caring and private and public practices of inner Peace;
• If we practice caring and inner/outer peace with self, others, and our Planet Earth we are
contributing to Peace in our world, through our individual and collective roles and actions.

Therefore, ON BEHALF OF THESE BASIC HUMAN CARING VALUES AND PREMISES, which
sustain human caring and contribute to peace in our world, WATSON CARING SCIENCE
INSTITUTE INTRODUCES THE INTERNATIONAL CHARTER FOR HUMAN CARING AND PEACE.

PLEASE JOIN ME AND NURSES AROUND THE WORLD BY
SIGNING YOUR NAME, AS YOU MAKE YOUR PLEDGE FOR
HUMAN CARING & PEACE.

**Watson Caring
Science Institute**

Jean Watson- International Charter Human Caring and Peace, for March, 2012 Hiroshima,
Japan Caring and Peace conference: Watson Caring Science Institute and Red Cross
University College of Nursing, Hiroshima, Japan.

The Caritas Path to Peace: A Guidebook for
Creating World Peace with Caring, Love, and Compassion

INTRODUCTION: USING CARITAS PROCESSES FOR PEACE

The Caritas Path to Peace will help you create a new world for peace by utilizing the 10 steps of the Caritas Process of Jean Watson's Caring Science Institute. These 10 steps have been used for many years to train nurses in hospitals to be caring, loving, compassionate caregivers. This book is revolutionary in that it uses techniques that have been used successfully with thousands of patients in hospitals to heal, to create personal and world peace.

This book is intended for people worldwide. Jean Watson's theory of human caring science is the foundation of the Caritas Path to Peace. Jean Watson has circled the world more than 12 times, bringing in the light of Caritas. She believes that Caritas can create an energetic field of peace worldwide- it can create "Caritas peace". "Caritas Peace" is a new concept that can change the world. This book is a calling to everyone to create a collective consciousness to bring peace into personal lives, peace to others, and peace to systems -- to create peace in the world. We are asking people to become peace activists and advocates, to commit themselves to being part of a ministry to create world peace. We are asking you to bring this light into the world, to the people they love, and to the communities they live in.

This book will give you the skills you need to be a Caritas peacemaker at home and in the world. It is a guidebook to take each of our lives as peaceful beings to a deeper level. First, this book invites you to become a Caritas peacemaker, second, it serves as a new paradigm workbook to help you follow through and do it. Using techniques from nursing care, psychology, healing, conflict resolution and wisdom traditions, this book will teach you how to make your life a peaceful life, at home, at work and hopefully in the world. With exercises, guided imagery, guidelines, and assignments, you can walk your own path to peace, beginning with yourself and moving on to the relationships in your life. Using the tools of Caritas, we will remake our lives and we construct a new reality.

All over the earth, people are making the choice for peace. Before the Iraq war, tens of millions of people from every walk of life marched for peace, to express their opinions and try to stop another war. For many of us, the Iraq war brought home the immediate urgency of changing paradigms, of being aware of our personal responses to violence, of and making peace a way of life. *The Caritas Path to Peace* is written for people worldwide who now believe in peace. We mean this book to be a contribution to the energy wave for peace that has risen all over the world. This book increases each person's ability to make creative solutions for inner peace and then for world peace. We want to empower the brilliant minds of those walking forward into the mystery of the future. We honor each individual who is working for peace; each person is part of a new unity, each is finding new solutions and new ways of being to change our world.

You have a choice for your future; you can move forward on a new path to peace- or you can turn back to the old path of conflict, violence, anger, and war. We refuse to go back to the habitual patterns of the human condition. We will seek solutions within ourselves, within our own wisdom. *The Caritas Path to Peace* will help you get in touch with your creative wisdom for peace.

JEAN WATSON'S 10 CARITAS STEPS TO CARING, LOVING AND COMPASSION

Jean Watson, at the Watson Caring Science Institute, has created 10 processes to guide us in implementing caring science in healthcare systems and hospitals. These processes are constantly changing-- organic and experiential. They provide us with the ability to articulate and create a language to shift our way of being. They are derived from the essential nature of nursing as proposed by Florence Nightingale a hundred years ago. They are from the clinical essence of what nurses are actually doing but don't often describe. They make the invisible become visible. In this book, the 10 Caritas steps will be our guide to living a peaceful life. This book will take you through the steps, chapter by chapter, in a practical, concrete, direct way to help you make peace.

Jean Watson's 10 Caritas processes are: (2012, changing and evolving

1. Cultivating loving kindness, compassion and equanimity with self and others.

2. Being authentically present, enabling the belief system and subjective world of self and others.

3. Cultivating your own spiritual practices beyond ego and self to authentic transpersonal presence.

4. Sustaining loving trusting caring relationships.

5. Allowing the expression of feelings, authentically listening and holding another person's story for them. _(story telling)_

   feelings – negative or positive

6. Creative solution seeking through the caring process. Full use of self with all ways of knowing/doing/being. Engaging in human caring practices and modalities.

7. Authentic teaching and learning- staying within the other's frame of reference, shifting towards a health coaching model.

   nurses _Educator_ _Connect_

8. Creating a healing environment- physical and non physical, a subtle environment of energy, consciousness, wholeness, beauty and dignity.

9. Reverently respecting basic needs, intentional caring consciousness by touching the embodied spirit of another as a sacred practice, working with life force of another- honoring the mystery of life and death.

10. Opening and attending to the spiritual and mysterious, unknown and existential dimensions of all vicissitudes of life,

death, suffering, pain, joy, transitions and life change -- allowing for a miracle.

As you can see, the steps do not depend on what political party you
vote for or whether you are conservative or liberal. They do not rely
on your belief in a specific war or your support of troops; they are
based on your hope for peace and come from the spiritual part of you
within. The techniques are based on the steps Jean Watson uses to
teach nurses loving and caring in hospitals; they come from many of
the world's wisdom traditions and from modern practices of psychology and conflict resolution. We believe that the path to peace starts
within. From inside, we move outwards. First we change consciousness; then we act. First we change our own consciousness; then we
change reality.

WAR IS THE ULTIMATE LIFE THREATENING ILLNESS

The Caritas Path to Peace is a book written by a physician and nurse
who have spent their lives using creativity and spirituality on patients
with life threatening illness. When we asked ourselves what we could
do for peace in this pivotal time, we realized that we could contribute
our knowledge of taking care of our patients who were very ill or
near death. In a very real sense, war is the ultimate life threatening
illness, and peace the ultimate life saving treatment and preventive
medicine.

We asked ourselves, "How do we take care of our patients with cancer
who may die? How do we bring back hope in desperate situations,
create change for healing, bring the healing power of spirit, and even
promote a miracle?" To answer those questions, we looked to our
research study at the University of Florida College of Medicine and
Nursing documenting how creativity helped heal patients with life
threatening illnesses. Mary's Arts in Medicine program at University
of Florida was based on Jean Watson's caring model. Our research
showed that creativity helped patients find love and compassion.
Our research showed that creativity helped each patient get in touch

with their inner wisdom, with their soul or spirit. This connection gave patients hope, rallied their bodies' own healing forces, and brought powerful healing forces from the universe to heal.

In the same way, creativity can help bring the energy of love and compassion to each of us to heal the life threatening illness of conflict and war. In writing this book, we found that we could often substitute the word "Caritas peacemaker" for "healer" or for "Peacemaker" in many of our guided imagery exercises. This in itself was a profound teaching. We realized that the Caritas peacemaker is a healer of the self, of relationships to others and to the world. When you make peace, you heal your own woundedness, you heal others with love, and you prevent more woundedness from being born. Creativity, love, and compassion are powerful tools for both healing and peace.

A powerful preventive medicine for the world is preventing war. What do we need to learn to stop seeing violence as a solution to economic and political problems? Man has fought wars for thousands of years. Wars kill tens of millions of people. Wars kill innocent women and children. In the twentieth century alone, wars killed over 200 million people. Isn't it time we stopped? Isn't it time we reacted to problems and crisis in a new way?

We started this book the day after 9/11. First it was called *The Path to Peace* and was about reacting to violence outside us in creative ways, with forgiveness and compassion. We worked on it for several months, then put it down and went back to our book *Shaman Wisdom, Shaman Power: Deepen Your Ability to Heal with Visionary and Spiritual Tools and Practices*. We picked up the peace book again as the Iraq crisis started becoming serious. Then, convinced that women were the key to peace and preventing war, we called it *A Gathering Of Medicine Women for Peace* and worked on it for several months. We put it down a second time to finish work on a project on how to use creativity and spirituality with patients at the end of life. We find ourselves picking this book up again in 2010 as the war on terror continues, the Iraq and Afghanistan conflicts continue, and other conflicts threaten in the world. This book is our offering, our ceremony, our gift, our work for peace. We can change our world for peace, it simply is time. This third turning of the Path to Peace into the Caritas Path to Peace is very beautiful and important for the world. We invite you to join us.

Join the world wide unity for peace, join the emerging global community of individuals who passionately believe in creative solutions for peace and for the end of war. The vision we all share and articulate is gripping, compelling, and beautiful. For the first time in history, millions of people share a vision of world peace. Even in these dark times, we see it, we feel it resonating in our bodies. Let's move towards it, let's gather together as a community to create this vision.

WE ARE THINKING AS ONE FOR PEACE

We are on verge of an extraordinary evolutionary step in humankind. For the first time in history, people all around the earth are communicating with each other in less than a millisecond. Without teachers, leaders, rules, laws or censorship, thought is moving freely around the earth like the air. The internet is the mechanism for this. Cell phones, facebook, and Twitter allow people to talk to other people in a millisecond, around the globe. Many thinkers have compared the internet to the theologian- philosopher Teilhard De Chardin's noosphere. The internet is in fact, a web of thought that surrounds the earth. Through the internet, cell phones and email, people are reaching out and speaking and listening to others around the earth. In one step, this is ending isolation and making propaganda more difficult to spread. Isolation creates fear and propaganda creates separation and dehumanization. Community and communication make it more difficult for leaders to manipulate us through propaganda and control of the media. For thousands of years leaders have made war the answer to their own political and economic self interests while they did not address the pressing social and economic problems that contributed to war.

Chardin had his realization about the noosphere after he carried stretchers with the dying and wounded in WW I. After facing the horrors of war he said, "No one can deny that a network (a world network) of economic and psychic affiliations is being woven at ever increasing speed which envelops and constantly penetrates more deeply within each of us. With every day that passes it becomes a little more impossible for us to act or think otherwise than collectively." Chardin believed that matter, and later life, is evolving towards a knowledge of spirit. He believed the noosphere was like God seeing himself or herself and was the emergence of pure conscious energy beyond the ego of one person acting alone for his own wishes. Chardin believed that this mega synthesis of the thinking elements of the earth towards a larger consciousness would result in a universal mindset which would take us beyond war and greed.

Humans are primates and the ancient primate territorial concerns have metamorphosized into material gain, control of energy resources, colonialism and religious fanaticism. The whole world can now see this clearly and is sick of it. Tens of millions of people all over the earth are now doing whatever they can for world peace. They act, even if they do not know what to do. They march, protest, light candles, block buildings, put their bodies in harm's way, build websites, write books, speak, teach, make art, volunteer, write email, sing songs, meditate and pray. They talk to people in other countries, friends and family, they appear on media, they express anger and they look for a new world without war. This has never happened before.

People are awakening to a new life of being people of peace. *The Caritas Path to Peace* is about conscious living, a new way of being, a new creative way of solving problems. We are each opening our minds and consciousness to think of something new and creative that has never been thought of before.. While we may not now have the conclusive answers to a particular problem, we can create a new a paradigm of creativity and find answers in peace. This will move humankind forward to a new way of being. Chardin believed the noosphere was a way of merging the oneness and connectedness of all people with the consciousness of God. He believed that all people seeing as one is nothing less than God seeing himself or herself. This is a very modern vision; it is the opposite of a leader wanting to wage war as one man to force another man to accept his own patriarchal god. *The Caritas Path to Peace* is the alternative to the path of greed, ego, control and power. It is the path of the universal consciousness of spirit.

We walk *The Caritas Path to Peace* by offering our own lives. One at a time, each person makes his or her life an offering to peace. Each person acts in simple steps to change her or his reality for peace. Together, we live in a consensual reality. The reality is a story, a construct. Together, we all consent to the reality. The reality has always been created by leaders, propaganda, life experiences and parental teachings. This constructed reality is called the "false self" by theologian Thomas Keating. A deeper reality of the true self or the God Self exists beyond this superficial reality. This reality is a reality of world peace, of evolution towards a higher consciousness where people accept each other with love. This is the new paradigm; and the tools of meditation, guided imagery, healing, commitment, creativity, spirituality and right action are the way to bring it to fruition.

We can offer our lives to shift the false consensual reality to the true reality. This is done through compassion, forgiveness, love, and prayer, and through our deep intention to change the way we live. When we make it our intention to live on *The Caritas Path to Peace*, action is born and the world is changed. Our life becomes a prayer for peace and the universe changes. When each person acts for peace, the leaders cannot continue to make war alone. We will consensually change reality and the world. We can and we will.

Peace is created with the energy of love and compassion. . It is an experience, an action. The ongoing crisis in Iraq has given each of us a new opening. Like an illness, it is a time for suffering, reassessment, and then readjusting priorities; it is a doorway to quick spiritual learning, and action. In illness and war, a person's energy changes in a moment, it is more spiritual, more intense and more alive. Cancer patients tell us, "There are no atheists in foxholes". They adopt this war metaphor to express a new spiritual conviction that comes to them with a life threatening crisis. When a person is near death he or she is more real, more in touch with a higher power then when he or she is doing something ordinary.

A war is a cry from mother earth to each of us. We hear it deep in our hearts. In this world, all is seen. The burnt children are seen, the bloody bodies of mothers are seen, the consequences of battle are seen. Even with the censorship and political takeover of American media, it is not easy to do things that are not seen by the world press. The people of the whole world are finally outraged by their leaders practice of solving problems with war.

Section One

EMPOWERING YOURSELF TO LIVE IN PEACE

CHAPTER ONE

THE INVITATION TO BE A CARITAS PEACEMAKER

WHO IS THE CARITAS PEACEMAKER?

There are people worldwide striving to create health and wholeness for the people they love. Peace is the fundamental foundation for wholeness and health. Caritas is an ethical and philosophical foundation for creating peace. People who love peace are everywhere. The Caritas peacemaker is the wise one who resides within each and every person. The Caritas peacemaker is the healer, the teacher, the lover, the giver, the mother, the father. The spirit of the Caritas peacemaker is deeply connected to the earth, to family, to friends, to animals, to the environment, to all of nature around us. The Caritas peacemaker can see the earth deeply; she can see the earth moving through her seasons. She can feel the wind, know when nature stirs, recognize the beauty inherent in the nature of life.

HOW DO YOU KNOW IF YOU ARE A CARITAS PEACEMAKER?

The Caritas peacemaker is the wise one within you who has a clear voice. She or he has spoken to you in your days of despair and pain. She or he was with you during your own birth and the birth of all your children. She holds strong, steady, and still. She has the ability to exhibit compassion, caring, wisdom and love in every aspect of life. These qualities come forth in relationships with others, in spiritual practice, and in all aspects of clinical work. The Caritas peacemaker is an archetypal position in our culture. The Caritas peacemaker stems from ancient times when women were herbalists, midwives, nurtures and healers. The archetypal Caritas peacemaker was worshipped as an aspect of the Goddess Hygeia. There have been many evolutions of this goddess throughout history from Hera, Isis, Athena, and Demeter, The Caritas peacemaker is involved in taking care of people or animals, tapping into the ancient traditions and wisdom of the past from the earth. The Caritas peacemaker is expanding beyond the traditional caring roles to include body workers, a mother, a father-- you may rub the body of a child after a long day; you may be a physician, a caterer, a pharmacist; all are your own ways of expressing the ancient peaceful nurturing knowledge within. The peace is in you as a vibrational energy which resonates in your body; the energy exhibits in individual ways since every woman and man is different.

Deep peacefulness comes to us like a dream, she appears in memories in our minds, she dances when we dance, she sings when we sing. She becomes stronger when we stand in a circle of other women and men who are peaceful people, who see each other and recognize each other and wake each other up. Peace is a state of mind, a state of body; the Caritas peacemaker within holds the fluidity of our spirit.

DEFINE YOUR AUTHENTIC LIFE AS A CARITAS PEACEMAKER

IF YOU ARE A CARITAS PEACEMAKER, YOU KNOW IT. YOU:

- Express peace as your truth.
- Honor peace in your body.
- Have a sense of purpose for peace.
- Interpret your visions of peace for the future.
- See more deeply into the comprehensive perspective of peace.
- Recognize the guardians on the path to peace
- See peace as around the corner.

Because you picked up this book, we know you are a Caritas peacemaker and change. We know you have the wisdom of the earth in your own body. You are connected to your own life, and you see what the world is about and what it is not about. With knowledge, we need to move forth and speak clearly to make peace. We need to move in the nurturing ways of the woman and the man supporting the woman. Our spirit is strong-- in rituals, in corporations, in business, our voice is strong. We need to go into our own personal lives and make a shift. Inside we need to step to the left and hold our body

Nursing!

5

in reverence and step to the right and use our voice in the world to make peace.

BASIC GUIDED IMAGERY EXERCISES TO VISION PEACE

Guided imagery is used in both seeing into visionary space and for moving energy. It is a tool used for changing reality and for spiritual growth. In ancient times it was not called guided imagery; it was called ecstatic journeying, or seeing into the spirit world. In the terms of modern psychology, the trance, altered states of consciousness, prayer, meditation and guided imagery are all ways a person sees into the intuitive inner world to heal. That is why it is probably easier for a modern person to become a psychic or healer-- these tools are deep in our culture; we can all learn them; they are part of our way of being already.

This book has guided imagery exercises to help you deepen your ability to see images, solve problems, and increase your own personal power as a Caritas peacemaker. The exercises have a defined form. The first part is abdominal breathing, the second relaxation, the third deepening. The fourth is the subject of the imagery, the intent and content. The fifth is the return to the room and grounding. The final step is an instruction for carrying something forward into your life. Each part is important, and as you get better you can shorten the introductions and closing somewhat if you wish. Each time you do a guided imagery you get better and better, and habits form. The relaxation takes place instantly after many practices.

To do the exercises, you can read them and try to remember and do them in your meditation space. You do not have to remember the exercise word by word, only the form; you can even make up your own words. Guided imagery is much more powerful when you make it up. Another thing you can do is have someone read it to you, make a tape and play it back. As you do more and more guided imagery exercises, you only need to read the content paragraph and let the rest come to you from memory.

IN YOUR MIND'S EYE

For all guided imagery exercises, make yourself comfortable. You can be sitting down or lying down. Loosen tight clothing, uncross your legs and arms. Close your eyes. Let your breathing slow down. Take several deep breaths. Let your abdomen rise as you breathe in, and fall as you let your deep breath out. As you breathe in and out you will become more and more relaxed. You may feel feelings of tingling, buzzing, or relaxation; if you do, let those feelings increase. You may feel heaviness or lightness, you may feel your boundaries loosening and your edges softening.

Now let yourself relax. Let your feet relax, let your legs relax. Let the feelings of relaxation spread upwards to your thighs and pelvis. Let your pelvis open and relax. Now let your abdomen relax, let your belly expand; do not hold it in anymore. Now let your chest relax; let your heartbeat and breathing take place by themselves. Let your arms relax, your hands relax. Now let your neck relax, your head, your face. Let your eyes relax, see a horizon and blackness for a moment. Let these feelings of relaxation spread throughout your body. Let your relaxation deepen. If you wish you can count your breaths and let your relaxation deepen with each breath. Then, gently let yourself return to your room. Move your feet and hands, open your eyes, and look around you. Feel your body; it is tingling, full of energy. This is the healing energy of peace.

A GUIDED IMAGERY FOR BECOMING A CARITAS PEACEMAKER

As you did before, make yourself comfortable. You can be sitting down or lying down. Loosen tight clothing, uncross your legs and arms. Close your eyes. Let your breathing slow down. Take several deep breaths. Let your abdomen rise as you breathe in, and fall as you let your deep breath out. As you breathe in and out you will become more and more relaxed. You may feel feelings of tingling, buzzing, or relaxation; if you do, let those feelings increase. You may feel heaviness or lightness, you may feel your boundaries loosening and your edges softening.

Now let yourself relax. Let your feet relax, let your legs relax. Let the feelings of relaxation spread upwards to your thighs and pelvis. Let your pelvis open and relax. Now let your abdomen relax, let your belly expand; do not hold it in anymore. Now let your chest relax, let your heartbeat and breathing take place by themselves. Let your arms relax, your hands relax. Now let your neck relax, your head, your face. Let your eyes relax, see a horizon and blackness for a moment. Let these feelings of relaxation spread throughout your body. Let your relaxation deepen. If you wish you can count your breaths and let your relaxation deepen with each breath.

Now in your mind's eye, see yourself as a Caritas peacemaker in your present life. See your body, the place you live, the place you do your work, a situation or people you are with. See yourself at home with your family, teaching children, dancing, speaking, doing ceremony. Let the peaceful way you are or will become come to you; see it in your mind, see it in detail, see it, feel it, smell it, hear it. Be there as a Caritas peacemaker. Now let yourself surrender to the process you are in. Give yourself fully to the process of becoming a Caritas peacemaker. Give your body, your life, as a sacred offering to the beloved work that you are doing. Realize that your work is sacred. Realize it is a gift to the community, and to the earth. Realize that you as a Caritas peacemaker are the hands of God. You hold the power of the whole system to heal. As you surrender, let yourself loose; relax deeper;, let yourself fall into the body of the beloved like you are diving into deep space. Do not be afraid, you are in the hands of God. You are weightless, falling into deepest space, surrendering to something much greater and older than your body and life in this single lifetime.

When you are ready, return to the room where you are doing the exercise. First move your feet and then move your hands. Move them around and experience the feeling of the movement. Press your feet down onto the floor, feel the grounding, the pressure on the bottom of your feet, the solidity of the earth. Feel your backside on the chair;

your weight pressing downward. Now open your eyes. Look around you. Stand up and stretch, move your body, feel it move. You are back; you can carry the experience of the exercise outward into your life. You will feel stronger and be able to see more deeply. You will be in a healing state. Each time you do the exercise you will be more relaxed, be able to go deeper, and become more deeply involved as a Caritas peacemaker in your life and in the world.

MANIFESTING THE CARITAS ENERGETIC FIELD : A VISUAL MEDITATION.

Instructions: Read this meditation in its entirety... then close your eyes for ten minutes to experience it energetically.

Find a place where you can be in silence and not disturbed a place away from ringing telephones, away from cell phones, away from visitors. Create a sacred space for yourself, allowing yourself to center and go inward to the world of your own heart and mind.

Begin by gently closing your eyes, taking slow deep breaths, allowing your body to relax, this is similar to the relaxation before a guided imagery exercise.

Now imagine in your mind's eye a small flame in the center of your heart. This flame is your life force; the flicker is the eternal flame of your being. It is life's sparkle. Focus on this light in the center of your heart. Alternate between seeing this and seeing out of your third eye in the center of your forehead. Begin to see out of your imagination; see through the eye in the center of your forehead, visualizing this flame in the center of your heart. This is the light of Caritas. Imagine this light beginning to glow more brightly, filling your entire chest. Feel the blissful nature of its radiant warmth and perfection. Allow this light to radiate through your entire body, illuminating the light in the mind's eye in the center of your forehead, all the way down to your sitting bones in your pelvis, the place where you are grounded. Imagine yourself as a burst of light, like a star being born.

As this is happening, to remain grounded, feel your earth connection through your body like a sense of gravity that holds you to the earth's energy. The earth is enveloping you like the jewel in the center of the lotus. Hold the flame of your life in place. You are the jewel in the lotus growing out of the earth. Feel your connection to the earth and the experience of being held. Now imagine the lotus growing within you and bursting into flames, becoming brighter as it travels up your spine. The lotus is blossoming as it travels up your body- up through your third eye to the crown of your head. As the lotus blossoms, the light from the Caritas energy field nurtures you. You expand; your consciousness is opening as you become the lotus of Caritas.

Sit with this image. You are sitting in the lotus, the lotus is blossoming within your body, and the lotus is growing out of the top of your head. Feel this connection between spirit and earth; you are the jewel that connects spirit and earth. You are the light of Caritas.

CHAPTER TWO

A PRAYER FOR PEACE ON THE EARTH

A PRAYER FOR PEACE ON THE EARTH

As we start as people of peace, as we start on the path of the Caritas peacemaker, we orient ourselves in the ways of the ancient journey. Native American wisdom traditions are wonderful teachers of spiritual techniques, attitudes and philosophies of peace. These wisdom traditions offer us the roots of spiritual healing, and techniques that resonate with our bodies.

The Iroquois nation of upstate New York had peacemakers come to them and change their lives from war to peace. As in ancient times, we look to the four directions to become oriented. From the directions come the energies of life and the guardians of the spirit.

We honor our ancestors who walked before us. Remember the time when we were all one family? We are children of common ancestors. Our ancestors tell us, "Do not war again." With the memories of the earliest times of humanity on earth, let us invoke the directions of the earth with the intention of making peace.

First, we call in the East – we call in the power of the rising sun, of new beginnings, of our most beautiful visions coming into light. We call in the air, the bird in flight, the power of feminine energy emerging in the world. We call to the East to empower our voices to speak and articulate our visions. We call forth the light of illumination as we begin to weave the web of feminine energy for peace. As we weave the web together for world peace, we will do things in new ways. We will remember the dawn of civilization, where we came from and where we began as one family. All people are our mothers, our fathers, our grandmothers, our grandfathers, our brothers and our sisters. They are.

Next, we call in the South-- we evoke the energy of manifestation. We remember humankind creating communities, cities, and progress. We see what we have created together in the light of day, we see technology, we see the good things. With the full noon sun, with fire, we stand tall, we speak out, we walk tall. We reclaim our authentic self in the light of day with confidence to bring forth our own voice. We will use the power of the life energy of creation to manifest life and not to destroy life.

Next we call in the West- we evoke the pure waters of interconnectedness. We honor the suffering and pain of our fellow humans. We remember we are all water, air, earth, and our dreams and visions. We evoke the element water to go deeper into our dreams, deeper into the darkness of our soul's embrace. We embrace our hidden self, our deepest suffering, in the darkness within, we hold pain and suffering like we hold our beloved. In the west we come from a place of our emotions; we let them flow deeply from the eternal spring of power. In the ending of the day, we go into our deepest dreams of peace.

Next we call in the North – we evoke the power of possibility, of potential for a new way of being. We evoke it from inside the void, the spaciousness where all things are possible. We evoke the abundance of the infinite potential in the cornerstone of power. In the north, the cornerstone of our power, we evoke the earth and the vastness of the universe. As the earth spins on its axis in the spaciousness of the infinite nighttime sky, we call forth the power of the universe to embrace all galaxies. Each woman holds in her uterus the great void from which all people were born. Woman gave birth to all humanity. Woman walks before us- mothers led us through wisdom- we women are holders of the void from which all things are born.

We call above to the air, upwards we evoke spirit. We look up to the sky, up to the infinite universe, open to mysteries, to the unknown, to spiritual presence. We ask our inner spirit to help us make peace.

We call down to the earth, downwards we evoke grounding. The earth grounds us in the diversities of the human species and animals. The earth grounds us in the seasons of our lives, in the ability of the earth to hold us and feed us. We thank the earth, our home, for the creative energy from which we live and grow.

Finally, we call inward to ourselves, we go inward on our journey for peace. We know peace begins in our hearts, in the opening of our own minds. As we start on this path as a Caritas peacemaker, we go within to center ourselves, to connect to the opening of our hearts and to the opening of our minds.

When we are oriented, we know where we are right in this minute. Now we can begin the journey on *The Caritas Path to Peace* - grounded, oriented, and in sacred space. With a sense of ourselves and of spirit we can move forward. We know that millions march with us; we are not alone.

EVOKE YOUR INTENTION FOR PEACE

In silence we make our intentions to create peace. We make our intentions with love. Go inward and get in touch with the love you have for yourself. Then, frame an intention for peace from your deepest love. Frame your intention carefully and say out loud or to yourself, "I invoke my intention for Peace. I invoke my intention for compassion, I invoke my intention for hope, I invoke my intention for silence, I invoke my intention for mercy." As you invoke your intention, you reveal your beauty. As you speak aloud, your inner beauty is revealed.

All our intentions weave together a web; all of our intentions spoken together form a cone of energy. We can raise the cone of energy for peace. Take your intention and gather it up and raise it over your head; take it up three times and offer it to the universe. Raise the energy, bringing together all the intentions all over the earth. Use drumming, rattling, dancing, or chanting to raise the energy.

CHAPTER: THREE

A GATHERING OF CARITAS PEACEMAKERS FOR PEACE

WILL YOU STAND WITH US?

The purpose of this book is to create a world wide gathering for peace. We see people worldwide as an important part of this project. We want to invite you to be part of this vision. We can do it in visionary space first, and then make it real in the world. It is time to gather women (and men) for peace. Will you stand with us?

This chapter is about Caritas peacemakers gathering for peace. You know who you are. In this moment, I reach out my hand to you; I open my heart to you. I can see who you are. Come stand up. Stand up for who you truly are. Stand up for the children of the world, standup up for the wisdom of the ancestors, stand up for your grandmother and grandfather, stand up for the mother- our earth. Stand up for the waters, the rivers, the oceans. Stand up for the nighttime sky, stand up for the beauty of the dawn, stand up for the air we breathe, stand up for the food we hunger for, stand up for life as we know it, and the life you want to see. As the big wild cats recede from the horizons of our landscape, you now hold within you the power of the great lioness. It is time to roar from your deepest dream. The world needs you now, so stand up. I am asking you to take your place as a caregiver, as a family member of a community. You are the ones we've been waiting for. If you don't do it, who will?

✗ THE HOPI ELDERS SPEAK

We Are the Ones we've been waiting for

You have been telling the people that this is the Eleventh Hour.

Now you must go back and tell the people that this is The Hour.

And there are things to be considered:

Where are you living?

What are you doing?

What are your relationships?

Are you in right relation?

Where is your water?

Know your garden.

It is time to speak your Truth.

Create your community. Be good to each other. And do not look outside yourself for the leader.

This could be a good time!

There is a river flowing now very fast. It is so great and swift that there are those who will be afraid. They will try to hold on to the shore. They will feel they are being torn apart, and they will suffer greatly.

Know the river has its destination. The elders say we must let go of the shore, push off into the middle of the river, keep our eyes open, and our heads above the water. See who is in there with you and celebrate.

At this time in history, we are to take nothing personally. Least of all, ourselves. For the moment that we do, our spiritual growth and journey comes to a halt.

The time of the lone wolf is over. Gather yourselves!

Banish the word struggle from your attitude and your vocabulary.

All that we do now must be done in a sacred manner and in celebration.

We are the ones we've been waiting for.

—The Elders Oraibi

Arizona Hopi Nation

TIME FOR THE WOMAN TO WALK IN FRONT

Thomas Banyacya spoke about women in the Hopi prophesy:

He said, "I'm going to talk about woman. You know a long time ago, I guess during a migration somewhere, {when they were} moving around to different areas, man used to walk up in front, with woman and children following him; he did that to protect them where they were going. Then later after they settled down, the man and woman walked side-by-side and the children followed them wherever they go. But now in the third period, women have a very important role to play at this time. It is time for women to walk up front."

He told in the Hopi language, that the woman stays up late trying to put baby to sleep. Maybe the baby's sick, wants to go to sleep. About two or three o'clock in the morning, when she wants to sleep, she goes down to the kitchen and cleans up the mess a little bit and then goes to sleep. And after about two hours she gets up again, starts cooking and puts on a nice table, cleans the table and tells the children," come and eat." All the children come and eat and rush off and leave the mess there. The mother has to clean up the mess again. That's another thing that needs to be stopped right now. He said the women should get to the rear of the husband and say, "Hurry up. Clean up this mess." That's what the Hopi said the women should do now. "We better get together and clean this mess up, because woman is going to be the producer of the next generation. What kind of a generation are we going to produce? What kind of life for the younger people? The woman is a representative of Mother Earth. Mother Earth is very shaky right now. And it's up to mothers now to really start looking into these things."

MEN WON'T ASK DIRECTIONS

There is a famous story women tell about men. "One day I was in a car with a man. We got lost. I saw he did not know where he was going. He wanted to drive, he did not want to ask anyone for directions. He told me he knew where he was going and he would get us there. He started to make wrong turns, kind of randomly searching for the destination as far as I could see. I knew where we were going; I have a uncanny sense of direction and can usually find a place intuitively. But, he did not want my suggestions, and I clearly saw I was not going to get where I wanted to go with him driving. I did not want to fight, so I relaxed-- and he did not get me there."

Women can often see visions of where they want to go. They can see the future deep inside of them; they can feel what will happen. The man will often act in the moment and the woman sees that is not what is supposed to happen. The woman sees and knows what is meant to be. It is time for change. Are you a woman who knows where she is going? If peace is your goal, can you see that the man is not going to get you there? Are you a man who realizes it is time to listen to a woman for directions to find a nurturing view of world peace?

A CALL TO GATHERINGS

One woman wrote this email after the crisis:

What can we hold onto? With burning buildings and screams of terror, the blanket's been pulled off. We are cold, chilly with fright. Expecting to get blasted with a little taste of history. United with our ancestral roots- for they too knew what it was like to live in fear. We ask ourselves in reflection if our dreams can remain alive, should we even try, or is this all futile? I ask myself as I stare out the window at the streams of patriotism blowing towards me, whipping in the wind, "why die for your country, instead of living for the world? America...so this is finding comfort in illusion". Since the blast, it seems like every day I wake up on the wrong side of the bed, or perhaps, like I had strange and disturbing dreams that have left a tainted residue of uncertainty surrounding me. Every breath I breathe reminds me not to look, but to see, this life embracing me...reminding me to embrace my life and all of the beauty in pleasure and the beauty in pain-I am ecstatic that I have

FEELING at all. Time to check my mental {state}, cross-referencing my past with my future potential. Can I really be the me that I see in my dreams? Or am I scared. You cannot hide from the sky, or whatever may fall from it; there is nowhere to run. So why live in fear of inevitability? The greatest fear is not that we might die. But that we might die without having done what we set foot on this earth to do, no matter what that might be. To question that perhaps you were a painter who has never held a brush, or a musician who never learned to read the notes. The hourglass has not gone dry. Breathe in. Breathe out. Regardless of whether bombs are showering down. Look to the sky with certainty. This is all happening for a reason. Learn. You chose this time to come to earth. There is purpose here for you to serve. Break free from the petty distractions that enchain you. Time stands still for the soul-searcher. Break down the barriers of your mind. Find the keys to enlightenment deep and divine. Life is too webbed and complex to wrap your mind around it...simply let it permeate your entire being...drenching your pores with experience. The way I look at it, you can either see the light in life...or wait and see the light that accompanies death. This is light that shines from within you...so you choose."

THE ANCIENT MOTHERS OF THE EARTH

Mary tells this story of meeting the ancient mothers of the earth.

I awoke early in the morning and entered the great Kiva in the Aztec ruin at dawn. I went down into the large kiva. I stood boldly in the center of the structure watching; the light shifted and the silence was full; it was that magical time in between the night and day. Then, in the shadows, I saw the ancient ones emerge. A circle of elders gathered around me. I saw an old grandmother, eyes sparkling. The rest of them were solemn and still and there was a heaviness and density in the room. The grandmother looked at me and while her mouth did not move, I could hear her voice. She seemed so familiar, as if she knew me. I felt she knew me on a level I did not even know myself. She spoke to me with great force: " You are one of the ancient mothers of the earth." Silence followed and I could feel all the eyes upon me.

Suddenly, I knew who I was. My body vibrated with energy. I heard it again: " You are one of the ancient mothers of the earth." I looked down at my hands and lifted them up into the air. I said to myself, "I am one of the ancient mothers of the earth." Now I was not afraid. My life had forever changed. I heard for the first time the fullness of my own voice. The elders gave me the gift of my own voice and in its wisdom I knew who I was in the world. I am an ancient mother. The next time I lifted my baby up, I realized it was true, I was really one of the ancient mothers of the earth, and all the ancient mothers of the earth were with me saying, "you are one of us."

MEDUSA RETURNS

Medusa transcends the women and she is the women. Medusa transcends the goddess and she is the goddess. Now Medusa is returning from the underworld, from her death, from her murder, from the amnesia of death. Everything is bombed, covered with fires; she comes up from the underworld where she has been dead. She is Medusa; she was killed by Perseus. As she crawls up from death, from the underworld, out of a crack in the earth, she emerges on a battlefield. She emerges covered with soot, with ashes of the burning of landscape. Her breasts are drooping. She finds a crying woman huddled with a child. The icons on her body were translated to icons of the devil. When Medusa saw the woman, Medusa saw the echo of what she was herself, the powerful and beautiful woman she had become on earth. She saw what was once a village and now was only a battlefield. She saw one lone whimpering woman abandoned with her children, , and she saw women walking over all the world with crying children in wars; she saw women everywhere.

Emerging she sees weathered tents; she hears whimpering. She sees an Islamic woman dressed in rags with a baby and a young child.

These are the first people she has seen. She looks in the eyes of a woman brutalized; she sees pain; she looks around and screams into the sky until her screams become as loud as thunder, and lightning bolts come down around her.

She has returned and she calls the rest of us to her, saying, "It has gone on too long."

We now are seeing our beloved earth as a battlefield; we see the earth open up; we see medusa crawling out from the underworld. She is huge, and as she crawls out we see the destruction of the earth from her eyes.

Medusa calls us with a different voice. In a different voice she calls the women and nurturing men together. She calls in a cry of sorrow and pain at the stupidity of killing. It is the same as the mother crying when her children are fighting; she always asks, "why are they fighting? Why does it have to be this way?" It is the sadness that goes on and on and on. It is her profound disappointment in humanity. It has not changed since she was killed thousands of years ago. Ten thousand years after Sumer, we still are killing for peace. Did you raise your child for war? It is time for this to end; we are more creative and innovative than that. It is time for the patriarchic colonial materialist model to end, and a world view of nurturing, ecology and peace replace it. We can do this. There are millions of us who want to do this.

GRANDMOTHER SPIRIT SPEAKS

For Native Americans, grandmother is the woman elder of wisdom. She is the holder of ancient female visionary space and she is also your grandmother healer ancestor. She speaks to us in this book now. She says:

"It is time to return to the work of the heart and the soul. This means, create sacred space to do action that is creative and healing in the world."

The ancient mothers of the earth gather now to stop war. Medusa returns now to stop wars and violence. Now is the time when women must lead, and men must listen. The ancient grandmother speaks to us now, listen to her voice:

"I see the women of the world. I see them while they do whatever they do as ordinary women. There has been a huge worldwide movement for peace in women's spirituality. I see the men in the world too. They know the time has come to change from patriarchal war to world peace and honoring the divine feminine.

"As women and men, it is time to make ceremonies all over the earth for peace. I have a vision of gatherings and ceremonies in Africa, Greece, Russia. The peace ceremony in Hiroshima for Caritas peacemakers is such a ceremony. (Jean Watson, 2011) I see women and men standing up, holding hands around world, virtually holding hands and actually holding hands.

"Listen to what I say: It is time to take your place and say, 'I am not putting up with this. I am in charge here. I am a powerful. I am going to include peace in my work now. I am strong and confident, I know who I am.' That is why I am calling for a gathering of women and Caritas peacemakers for Peace. It is time to gather the ancient medicine women who are now Caritas peacemakers for Peace; and we are standing up, changing the earth, as woman not men.

As we stand together in a sacred circle, we stand with all the ancient grandmothers of the earth; they stand before us and behind us. In this sacred circle there is an interconnectedness, and we stand as one. It is time to take your place in this ancient sacred circle. Stand, announce yourself and present yourself in this circle. As you do this, together we reclaim the divine feminine. This action is essential to honor ourselves and others, and create peace in the world.

I had a vision of a world gathering for peace. I saw millions of women, the women and children in the center, the men outside, just standing and holding the space, creating sacred space, not moving. We

Lnurses & patients
Nurses & their leaders   23
Leaders & self
one

took the women from the center, we spiraled around the children. The women began to move; the men still held the space.

patients & staff

In the beginning, we celebrate, honor, thank and appreciate the men for contributing. We thank them for committing to help. We thank them for creating our lives, building cars, airplanes, buildings. Then we ask them to stand still as we spin the medicine wheel for world peace. The children are our gift to the world, our gift of new life. They are the new dream, they play in the center of the circle. Then we bring in the energy.

We make a heart of world peace inside the circle, we play, women hold hands and spin and dance for world peace. The ceremony is huge. It is a gathering of the women committed to a vision of world peace."

Then three owls called. The grandmother's vision was complete.

A WOMAN'S DREAM OF HEALING THE EARTH

A woman with chronic rheumatoid arthritis told us how upset she was because of the world crisis. After talking about her ups and downs, her fears and depression, she told us this dream:

"I was sleeping. I then found myself in a light tunnel. I thought it was an ice tunnel, but I realized it was made of soft luminescent white light. I floated upwards in this beautiful tunnel and came out of its end. It was like a flower, it felt like I was like being born. I was in deep space, floating. I was connected to earth with a silver thread that came from my belly button. The source of power was off to my left. I was afraid of it and stayed away. I saw the earth below. It was sickly, the bottom part was dark, smoky like it was on fire. I let my energy down and it healed. It become green and soft again, then full of light. Finally I was the earth, my body turned into the earth and we were one. When I healed the earth, I healed my arthritis, we were one."

This dream is a woman's dream of connectedness, of being the earth. It is a dream about her healing the earth, about knowing what to do and doing it. It is a dream about astral travel and energy and healing. It is what women know now. It is an accurate dream about what she needs to do now. It is her part in this crisis. She is a woman healing the earth in this crisis.

WOMEN JOIN TOGETHER

Our reaction as women needs to be timeless, men talk about details, current events. What is happening in the world is scary, violent; this isn't going to work. It is not working. This is affecting women, men, and children all over the world;, they see that it is not about war, it is about peace and wisdom. It is about tapping into the wisdom of our souls, knowing in our deepest self that we are truly capable of love and forgiveness. And then it is about taking care of what we need to take care of, our children all over the world.

If you hold fast to your belief it happens. We are Jedi knights, we can use the force- the force here is mental control and intention to create world peace. *Intention to create peaceful spaces*

I see the Kitchen Committee in Europa, women in charge. Men sit getting ready for war, with chants, while women make food and take care of children, tend the sick, create home, men doing nothing but war. This once was the biological imperative; it does not work anymore. Join together in a new way for peace.

This chapter is not about the gender of women exclusively; we are not excluding men in any way. We honor, appreciate, and see men. But the next evolutionary step is to be taken by a feminine energy and male energy merged together, not male energy alone. Male energy alone is a force with techniques to kill and make war. That energy needs to be stilled to allow the energy of the feminine to expand and grow. A rebalancing of energy is necessary right now. *Respect*

Wait, men-- don't move now, look and see what is happening. It is a time for women to reach out over the darkness and see who is the enemy. We need to see-- is there something we have done? We need to look inward as well as outward. We know this. We need to take responsibility for our actions or inactions, to listen and see what has been done and hasn't been done for starving people. The most important thing needed now is food. Do we need to kill these people or feed them? We are dealing with the male patriarch at its zenith. It is time for women to stand up. We know the Afghan women, we know them through our own fears; we remember when it happened to us. It is happening to us, if we don't do something different. If male energy is allowed to perpetuate this, it will happen to us. We too will be stripped of our own dignity. Nothing is changed, those who stay home are still not valued, we have no economic value as we raise his children for war. Unless you do a job in the male world you still have no value.

Women and men: Go into a room, do a ritual in your psychic space. Do a ceremony, do a chant, light a fire. Move out of the male energy. Wake up! Something unusual has happened. I stood up and I was not who thought I was. I am not predictable, so excitement and stimulation arises. I want to bring people to the place in their own visionary space where they can have an opening. I want you to have a flood of emotion in being with yourself, in hearing your own inner words reverberate with a vibrational tone within.

FEMININE LOVE IS KNOWING INSTINCTIVELY WHAT ANOTHER NEEDS

This story of a woman awakened by her baby crying in the middle of night is familiar to every woman: You feel your baby cry before your baby starts to cry. There is anticipation which moves you out of deep sleep, and suddenly you awaken and listen. There is a moment of silence; then you hear a tiny squeak, the sound of moving. Your baby starts to cry. You anticipate the crying. You feel it in your breast, your body. You begin to feel another human reaching out for you. When you wake up, it's silent except for the crying. You hold your baby to your breast. Your baby reaches with her tiny mouth, her tiny fingers, helpless and beautiful. She searches for what she needs. You hold her, breathe in your baby's smell; you feel her hair, her softest skin. In a moment you feel a connection deeper than primal. It is the connection to life. Your arms hold life without judgment, without knowing who she will become. In that moment there is ancient memory. All humanity is like that baby; every person had that experience or didn't have it. Every person had the comfort of being loved by the mother.

The world needs the tenderness of a woman instinctively loving in life. She takes care of life. Men are caught up in words. She makes it possible for life to happen. The man can learn from the woman's embodied intuitive ability to love. He can watch and learn to feel and anticipate needs of a lover and a child. He can learn to be nurturing and caring. Many men today have learned this lesson and are ready to move forward in a new way for world peace. The woman is our teacher. As the mother, as the primal caregiver, she is the symbol of nurturing. The earth needs this way of being to survive.

⌐ Nurses, Leaders, Self

THE LEGEND OF THE STEALING OF THE RATTLE

There is an ancient legend of the birth of the patriarchy. It tells of a women's circle in ancient times. There, tribal women in the woods gather flowers, make food, fabrics, clothes, herbs, fire, baskets. They also make rattles for their babies. A woman told this story. "The men watched from a distance. They saw us talking, touching and laughing. They were jealous; the men thought we were powerful, as we gave birth to the babies. That gave us control. One day, the men came quietly through the jungle. They watched us as we laughed and played, milk coming out of our breasts. The men desired us,; they said we had the secrets of life. The men sneaked up and stole the rattles. We laughed and made believe the rattles were magic. The men watched. We laughed because they were baby rattles and the men thought they had power. Then the men took it all. They took the rattles, the nakedness, the earthiness. Our power became forbidden after it was stolen. We made believe it was magic and they stole it."

The ascendance of the patriarchy and collapse of the matriarchy has reached the zenith in modern warlike cultures. Men control the military and make decisions for war. Women and children are victims. It is time this way of looking at the world stopped. The rattles were baby toys. The bombs and rockets that replaced them are not.

We are not going to war. We are going to put women in charge and see what happens. We are going to put women in charge for change. Not women who are like men, not women who think like men, who have become like a man. We will put a woman who is loving, nurturing, and feminine in power. A powerful woman who is a woman in her power. A woman has a male side; she can see the part of herself who is aggressive, who protects her children. A woman can be like a female bear who protects her cubs, but she does so only when threatened--she is a powerful animal. Now women must stand and fight off the enemy by moving past the animal way of being. We talk about power, use bear energy for power, but also have compassion, love, and the wisdom of a human woman. Finally we have evolved past primal aggressive animals.

We are something more. This is our chance to experience what the real potential is for a human. This is the time to experience being the enlightened creature we have become.

It is really time for the woman to walk ahead. In the past, man walked ahead to protect the woman and children, but now that is actually more dangerous as he leads the women and children into war. Now one man can kill thousands, not just a few as in ancient times. Perhaps we could let him do this then, but we cannot let him do this now.

This book gives us a method for a woman to create world peace. It gives every woman concrete practical steps to walk the way of the Caritas peacemaker. The method is a practice. You do it by being who you are. It begins by saying to yourself in a commitment, "I am willing

negative ← & → positive

to do this, I am not willing to do that. I am being true to my feelings in my body and my heart. I honor the wisdom in my body. I honor the wisdom in my heart. It is about standing up for yourself and what you believe in, standing up for peaceful solutions, standing up for a peaceful world. The way to world peace is to be yourself, true to your feelings. Let your wise woman speak in your own life, in your work, & family, and actions.

Nursing Science versus & Medical Model

TAKE A LONG WALK AS A WOMAN

Take a long walk down a winding road. Let the wind blow in your face, feel your body moving through time, take in the sensual experience of being alive. Make a commitment in the deepest place in your soul you can reach. Be open like the open woman; everything flows through her.

There is a woman inside of me-- I can feel her echo of ancient lovers, she is a visionary mystic. I feel her existence. I see her face, she opens up our heart. I let her go in. Her spirit comes inside me… I become large. Spirit is separate, in service to spiritual beings… she is the manifestation of love. She is the manifestation of the earth mother, the pregnant fairy woman. She is a real spirit looking for and returning to spirit. I stand behind her and go forward when all we have to do is go inward.

Create the open woman, open wide, let her voice come through you, otherwise outside of your self. I open my life to allow our love to flow into my life… I do not close anything, I open it up. It does not define any place in the external world for love to flow. I open within myself and movement of love begins to flow from within….connects me with god and the rhythms of the earth

(Nursing)

In love, the most important thing you can do is open your lives to each other and to the creative flow that comes into us… it keeps flowing.

TIME TO CHOOSE YOUR PATH : WALKING THE PATH OF ANGELS

In our lives, we have two choices of paths to walk: we can walk the worn and weary path to war or walk the less traveled path to peace. The path to war is the way man has walked for thousands of years. The path to peace is the way woman will walk for thousands of years more. *The Caritas Path to Peace* is not the well worn path, it is a path only angels have treaded. You can't see their footprints- you must make your own.

Peace in Nursing!!!

THE HOPI PROPHESY

The Hopi Indians from Arizona have an ancient prophesy that is part of their creation myth. A Hopi elder Thomas Banyacya was told by a group of elders in 1948 to share the prophesy with non-Indians for the first time. Thomas himself was a conscientious objector; he was jailed for five years for refusing to fight in World War II. During his life he fought for the environment and for peace. He lived his beliefs fully.

The Hopi prophesy tells us that we are at a critical time in history. The Hopi elders tell us that we have reached a fork in the road of the future. There are now two paths that are open before us. The first is a path of the technology that is separate from natural and spiritual law- - this path leads to chaos. The second is a path that remains in harmony with natural law. Each person must choose which path to walk. If we walk the path of spiritual harmony and live from our hearts, we can experience paradise in this world. If we walk only on the path of technology and war, we will come to destruction.

The Hopi teaches us that this is a time to weigh our choices for our future. If we, as people of the nations of this Earth, create another great war, the Hopi prophesy is that we humans will burn ourselves to death and turn into ashes.

But the prophesy tells us that there are two paths. We do have a choice. The choice is how we lead our life; it is each decision in our

Unions & Nursing

Choose a road and walk!

very way of being. The choice is in each of our thoughts, our prayers, our work, and our actions. *Daily living, Work. morning huddles*

When Thomas Banyacya taught the prophesy he said that now is the time for every person to choose the path they will walk. Up to now, the choice has been for the Hopi people, and now it is for non Indians as well. He said that each person must choose fully and completely. Each individual must totally commit their whole life to the choice- to walking the path for peace- or we as humans will not survive.

Banyacya taught that each individual must walk the path regardless of the outcome. Each of us must walk the path for peace with our whole lives, our full power – as if the path was certain. Whether or not the path for peace is the one that prevails, certain people are destined to walk this path with full commitment. This is their destiny, this is who those people are. *Be confident - you chose the right path!*

The Caritas Path to Peace is our full commitment; it asks you to make your full commitment to the path of peace. *Peace in Nursing*

THIS IS YOUR CHANCE TO MAKE A CHOICE.

We are at the turning point where we can shift the entire world's consciousness. We have reached a crisis which demands that each of us make an internal choice for peace. The impact is enormous- all of us are standing at the threshold--some know this and others have not yet figured this out. The peace marches of millions of people show us that there already are many of us walking together. This book connects you to your own heart and to the millions who stand with you. We don't know the creative ways it will manifest but we know that as we stand together, we can move forward in space and time with our lives and bring peace. As we are in conversation with others in contradiction; this is the moment to have faith, be confident. Know that it is you who will make a difference. If it weren't for you, there would be no peace movement. It is about one human being at a time casting the net for peace.

chaos

Be clear; this is your chance to make a choice. The first choice is to continue to live in hatred, pain, darkness, fear, anger, and revenge. The second choice is to live in love, forgiveness, compassion, power, and prayer.

Choice gives you a path to a deeper understanding, a path to a personal way of being rather than a political way of being. It is time to take a new step that has never been taken before, an individual step to create peace, harmony, and balance in our world. We need to have greater personal protection, but it must come from a place of social justice, equality and respect. It must come from the greater and more sustaining strength of the power of nurturing and love.

There is one choice: mother earth, habitats, balance and harmony vs. poverty, starvation, war and greed. It is a choice between acting out of fear or acting out of love, acting out of creativity or acting out of revenge.

Actions = true self

You can make the choice now to act out of love. To do this, watch your own actions and discover who you really are. In that way you can act to save the earth for seven generations to come. It is not about countries being against countries any more, we are a global world. Within that world there are individuals who have fallen. We must find them and have compassion for them; as we protect ourselves, we must forgive them, include them, and hold true to our hearts.

To begin the choice, let God's love and light come forth within you. While he was dying- while he had nails in his hands- Jesus said "Forgive them- they do not know what they do". Jesus never hit anybody back. He never fed the energies of hatred and war. He put all his energy into forgiveness, peace and compassion. We tell our children not to hit back, we put them in a time out. We need to put our leaders and the warlike men in a time out. *↳ Administrators / CEOs*

Many peoples from many cultures have had prophesies about the future. They usually go something like this: A time would come where each person would have to make a choice in their own lives between what they saw as good and what they saw as evil. They would be up against the wall. In the prophesies, our lives are our spiritual path. Our lives are a challenge for our spirits to grow and evolve. Seeing another as evil and wanting to destroy him is the challenge; learning to see the other with compassion and learning to understand him is the answer. Each experience of suffering or physical pleasure, each experience of pain or joy, of sorrow or happiness, of anger or love is a teaching. Each experience releases feelings of revenge or compassion, of rage or love. The experiences of our lives on earth give us feelings in every moment. And… in every moment we have choice. Every circumstance, every encounter, is another time for a choice. The prophesies say that the future is determined by how many people choose which reality. Some prophesies foretell the end of the world. Even those prophesies say that the people who choose peace must do so no matter what the outcome appears to be. Other prophesies foretell a paradise for those who live in love and peace. When we live in peace, our paradise is now. Our spirit lives in a moment of love and experiences love as reality.

MARY'S STORY OF 9/11

How are you reacting to the world situation now? Mary tells her story of her reactions to 9/11:

"After 9/11, I had no doubt who I was, I was not confused. The second it happened, I felt hurt, pain, sadness, and fear. I also reacted with feelings of peace and forgiveness. I yearned for a creative solution that would not cause war. Every time I heard the cries for war, for revenge, I felt it was a disproportionate reaction; I became filled with sorrow.

I felt a swift sureness in my heart of what would be the thing to do. It confused me how powerful the image was… we were attacked and there was such pain and outrage to my body, to my country, to the earth,. My first impulse was to be stunned, and ask "Why would anyone do this? What were they trying to accomplish? Did I miss something?" I believed in my heart that we as Americans were a people of greatness. We are a melting pot of the global community, a majestic people blessed with prosperity, good fortune, and safety. I had a feeling of the strength of who we are. Then I felt, we must protect ourselves.

What I realized next was that in being so blessed, we as Americans needed to be very large and see beyond ourselves into the new millennium and do something radical that had never been done before. In that moment was a window to deepen our understanding of ourselves and what impact we had in the world. We needed to understand what we did not know and forgive ourselves for what we may have done. We also needed to forgive them for their attack. I was aghast and my desire was to reach out over the ocean to understand how this could have happened. We need to make a gesture to heal the world. I thought, what can I do in this moment when we have been assaulted, to bring world peace? I felt tears in the depth of my soul, I felt a powerful compassion towards victims-- first to the people in the plane, next to those in the building, then the fireman... and then the people we had afflicted harm on that felt the need for revenge. I spent the next days dealing with my own feelings. Others around me seemed twisted with hatred. It seemed that as the act was violent with hatred-- we were reacting with violence and hatred too. It seemed to me that if we were not careful, we would turn into what we were afraid of. I could see that each person was coming to a crossroads in her or his own life.

As I looked at my own life, I began to see why I reacted as I did. My story was very much the story of a woman. I began to understand why women react to peace and war differently than men, because in my personal life I have been raped, physically abused, abandoned and my voice repressed. And because of that I have come to a place of my own inner conviction.

As a little girl of seven years old, I lived in Turkey, immersed in the Muslim world. My father was a Lt. Colonial in the Air Force. He was a diplomat and an advocate for the middle east international relations. He represented the Turkish point of view in the conflict between

Turkey and Cyprus, for U.S. military intelligence. As a child of a military officer, I spent most of my life abroad.

In WW II my father liberated one of the concentration camps in Germany. When I was a little girl, he took us to the camp and showed us the horrific consequences of human ignorance, cynicism and cruelty. As a child I felt myself a part of a global world, but I always was American. I felt lucky with my liberty and prosperity and justice for all.

But then came the sixties, and another event that formed who I was happened in the American south. The Klu Klux Klan burned a cross in front of the house of a black girl I knew. She was in my fifth grade class, and she was my friend. She told me what it was like to have rocks thrown in the front door and through windows of her home. She huddled behind furniture in total fear, surrounded by hatred. She asked me, "What do they hate?" I looked at her and was stunned and confused, I did not understand.

My personal experience of pain and violence continued as a teenager in high school. During the race riots, I was viciously beaten and kicked and stuck with pins by eight black girls. I was trapped inside a bathroom in the school being beaten when a huge black boy came in, chasing the girls away and rescuing me. He picked me up in his arms and carried me to the ambulance and saved me. In the chaos, I was feeling being hit and attacked and at the same time carried and saved-- by the same people. The white students wanted to hunt and beat up the girls; they came in my front door. This was not what I wanted to do, and I stopped them

As a young teenager, I was in a relationship with a boy where I was repeatedly abused. I believed love healed everything; this was not the case. Just loving someone did not necessarily change things; it was a powerful lesson. Over the time I was with him, I was beaten, I was raped, I was thrown over a balcony which broke my back and broke my arm. I was stalked for months on end and fell into a spiral of the fear of being beaten, trembling when I was alone. An aggressive prosecutor wanted to put him in jail, he wanted me to press charges. I did not want to send another human to jail, and would not help him. I learned from this abuse that love does not necessarily change the other person-- but acting out of love does heal your own life. Forgiving someone will allow you to let go and let your life go on. Forgiveness frees you to move on and accept your own pain and suffering, and move beyond without being stuck in the past.

Many years later, when I was in the midst of a painful divorce process, I was hysterical and fighting. My husband had left me and abandoned me with two young small children. I was in despair and experienced an uncontrollable anger. After the fight raged, my own body was bloodied, and I saw that all my anger did not get me anything. The rage and anger just hurt me more deeply. I saw that in every battle, I came out more wounded than before. I realized that all that happened was I would explode and go nowhere. I realized that the essence of life was taken from me. Instead of the pain being inflicted on me by others, I was inflicting it on myself. I realized that I needed to forgive myself for my own rage. I finally let go of wanting something I could not have, and believing the world would accommodate the dream of what I wanted it to be. In the midst of this letting go and forgiveness, one day my husband knocked at the door and asked me if he

could come home. In my heart, I made a decision. He came home and the power of forgiveness was born within me.

In one day, my whole life changed. I made a commitment to be on a spiritual path, to choose the path of love, compassion and forgiveness. I didn't know what that path was, but each life experience had become a thread which led me within my life to it. I realized then that my life had become a challenge, a test. This is a commitment to a way of being, not necessarily to a way of understanding. Things can be too complex. I can commit to a way of approaching or moving away from something, not necessarily to understanding everything and coming to a conclusion. As you move forward in your life, as forgiveness becomes embodied, it resonates with the core essence of who you are. Now it's about having faith in yourself. You can call forth the strength of this experience and move forward.

The crisis of 9/11 reminded me that my life was at a turning point. My life lessons have accumulated to be something that emerged in that moment. They are not a philosophy or a discourse but a personal experience of what had worked for me and what hadn't worked for me. I realized that my own life was the lesson that led me as a woman to forgiveness and compassion. Women who are abused and abandoned must get past all of the pain to grow into a new future. Women need to turn the experience of abuse into their desire for world change.

REFLECTIONS OF PEOPLE ON THEIR OWN LIVES

Your lived experience of your own life has made you who you are. Your past lives have made you who you are. How has your life taught you spiritual teachings? How have you learned forgiveness and compassion? A crisis activates the spirit of compassion in some of us. At the end of every war, the warrior needs to become a healer; the horrors of war need to be healed.

Your own story is your personal path to understanding and forgiveness. In the changing world, you can look at your own life as your teacher. It leads you to your turning point. In the crisis your life is what makes you react.

TELL YOUR OWN LIFE STORY AS A CARITAS PEACEMAKER

What are the lessons you learned in your own life? Who are you? What is your commitment to being a spiritual person in this planet? What do you believe when you stand against people? If it is hatred you need to be honest. That is the path you are on.

Look at who you are, accept it, honor it, be it. You are not alone in your conviction of world peace. Strengthen your conviction of being on the road to peace. Be the peaceful warrior, wear no armor, take up no arms. Write your life story down from the point of view of the Caritas peacemaker, of compassion and love. See who you are and how you got here.

I stand vulnerable before you. I say, life, flow through me, I am vulnerable... I feel pain and sorrow... life flow through me. I am part of the river of life. When I gave birth to my child, I gave birth to death. I am large enough to embrace both. I am the voice of a woman.

THE PEACEFUL SOLUTION

We have the ability to act differently because we are stronger. We have the ability to act differently because we live in a democratic way of government. In our history, we have abolished slavery, we have dealt with diversity. We have been the first people to do so many things.

Now we have the opportunity to be the first people to act with peace and forgiveness in a crisis. Imagine what world history would say: "They were attacked and they acted in forgiveness. This was the first time in history that happened. They created the new era of world peace. This breakthrough was the most important moment in history. They learned about those who attacked them and worked with them to resolve problems and create prosperity and peace." We have the capacity—and the opportunity-- to do the right thing. This is a deeply spiritual country; we can act with peace and forgiveness instead of reflexively acting out of war. We can be a people of real spirituality, not religion in the name of war for personal greed. The God of revenge, fear and war was described in times of tribal war. This is not my God. This was not Jesus' God. (?) Jesus = God

A crisis is a quandary; it poses a problem that must be solved. It is a situation which releases a deliberate response in each of us. The response can be a creative solution which forgives, heals and makes peace, which feeds the hungry, offers apologies, and makes a new world. It can be a response of love and compassion. This is a new way of reacting to any crisis situation in our life. It is a new way of reacting to all situations. *The Caritas Path to Peace* is just as applicable to a relationship, a business quarrel, a death of a loved one, as it is to war.

There has always been violence in the world. We suggest that for the first time humankind can react to violence and death with acceptance and love. That does not mean we do not protect ourselves. We can fight back with nonviolence like Gandhi. We suggest that humankind can react consciously with intent and commitment to peace. People can make the choice, say what they are doing, do it with intent, and change the world forever.

Conflict = change

We have a choice-- anything is possible. In any moment a new consciousness can be born on earth. Each moment is pregnant with change. In this very moment lies the ability to make a quantum leap in human history. This is a chance for a whole new paradigm to be born. Each of us can give birth to a new way of seeing, a new way of being, and a new way of loving on earth.

A crisis produces a massive shift in consciousness; this is happening right now. Some react with a reflexive call to war. That is a natural reaction. Then time changes things, and more and more people react with a creative path to peace. The next steps we take are critical. You are not alone; we are together. A group of people on this planet is reacting differently. Like a star cluster we will illuminate the universe with peace in mystical space-- like a nebula. This is actually happening now. We live within a web of life… we live with animals and the earth. The rivers, air, and animals are part of this complicated web; they are not interested in war. We need to act as a species to prevent environmental damage to habitats and the earth…to act in harmony and balance with the rest of life on earth.

BOLDLY GO

All over the earth, people are working for peace. People go the war zones and volunteer; people go to places with violence and natural disasters. Nurses, women, medicine women, sacred healing priestesses, oracles, dreamers- boldly go and manifest the new reality. In the gathering of women, come together, see each other, make community, combine your powers. Change reality as one huge force of nurturing feminine energy. This is a new time… suddenly the woman is called to come forth, but she is called as medicine woman, the healer, the oracle, the priestess, the Goddess as one with the God- to change the earth again, to reestablish balance.

Make your commitment to be a woman who changes her world, her family's world, the world. Be a woman who heals herself, others, and the earth. Be a woman who changes the consciousness of the earth from reflexive male war to world peace, . Women do not go to war; woman holds sacredness.

Men, medicine men, sacred healing priests, oracles, dreamers- boldly go and manifest the new reality. In the gathering of men, come together, see each other, make community, combine your powers. Change reality as one huge force of masculine energy combined with feminine energy. This is a new time… suddenly the man is called to come forth, but now as medicine man, the healer, the oracle, the priest, the God as one with the Goddess- to change the earth again, to reestablish balance.

Make your commitment to be a man who changes his world, his family's world, the world. Be a man who heals himself, others, and the earth. Be a man who changes the consciousness of the earth from reflexive male war to world peace. Nurturing men do not go to war; he holds sacredness together with her.

CENTERING PRAYER AS A TECHNIQUE FOR PEACE

Before Jean speaks to a gathering of Caritas peacemakers, she uses a singing bowl calibrated to the heart chakra. She gently begins to play the singing bowl and the singing bowl creates a sacred sound. As she gently plays the singing bowl, the room becomes quiet and focused. She pauses, and she becomes an energetic field of Caritas. She uses the sound and the presence of her body to hold sacred space. As she stands in front of the room, she silently calls for silence. In the silence she stands and fills the room with her presence. Her presence radiates love, power, peace, and compassion. Her presence is an inspiration for everyone to pay attention and be still. Each person in the room begins to settle in their body and she requests for people to close their eyes and become centered. Her words guide people, her words relax people, her words open their hearts to receive the wisdom of Caritas. She stands in the light holding the radiance of the Caritas energetic field and all hearts begin to beat as one. When she speaks, people hear their own heart speaking. They recognize she is one of us who has remembered who we truly are. She speaks softly; people become centered, they connect to themselves. As she speaks, the gathering becomes collective consciousness; as each nurse focuses on their heart, all hearts become one Caritas energy field, and that is how gatherings begin.

Jean Watson does a centering prayer each time she opens up her presentations on Caritas. She creates a pause in which she calls us to remember our heart's intelligence. Her gentle words invite us to close our eyes and simply center, pausing. This is an energetic shift to embody the wholeness of Caritas in every cell of your being, opening the heart to feel and see and be. *Nursing - feel, see & be*

THE TECHNIQUE OF CENTERING PRAYER

Keating developed centering prayer as a method to hear the voice of God within. It perfected the technique partly to give Christians an equivalent of Eastern meditative techniques, which were attracting many people away from the church. Based on ancient Christian ways of prayer, centering prayer is a practice, not a doctrine. In centering prayer, the person sits comfortably and closes her or his eyes. The person chooses a sacred word as the symbol of her or his intention to consent to God's presence and action within. She or he then settles briefly and silently introduces the sacred word into consciousness. When the person becomes aware of thoughts, she or he returns ever-so-gently to the sacred word. At the end of the prayer period, the person remains in silence with eyes closed for a couple of minutes. Many readers will recognize the similarity of centering prayer to eastern meditation techniques.

Thomas Keating, a Trappist monk and author of *Centering Prayer,* defines a false self as "an image developed to cope with the emotional traumas of early childhood which seeks happiness in satisfying the instinctual needs of survival and security, affection and esteem, power and control." This false self starts in childhood and develops as the child is frustrated by not having his or her needs totally met. When a need is frustrated, the need turns into a large drive in adulthood. For example, when the need for security is frustrated, the adult is always insecure and spends time trying to be protected from dangers which may or may not be real. If the child is frustrated in power and control, the adult wants to control others-- a company, a country. If the child is frustrated in both sur-vival and security and control and power, the adult needs to pro-tect himself with war and to control the world. Does this sound familiar? One theory about a leaders such as George W. Bush is that he is attempting to meet massive unmet needs of childhood by acting them out in the adult world. This is one belief about the basic cause of war.

From Keating's point of view, massive unmet needs of childhood can never be satisfied by adult acting out. The only way to meet these needs and to heal is to connect with something larger than the per-sonality, with the voice of God. The way to heal is not to listen to voice of the false self which only attempts to answer the unfulfilled child-hood needs of security and control, but to listen to the true voice of the soul which tells the person that they are loved by God. This finally heals by giving the person lasting feelings of security and control which go far beyond childhood needs.

CENTERING PRAYER TECHNIQUE

- Sit comfortably and close your eyes.

- Choose a sacred word as the symbol of your intention to consent to God's presence and action within.

- Settle briefly, and silently introduce the sacred word into consciousness.

- When you become aware of thoughts, return ever-so-gently to the sacred word.

- At the end of the prayer period, remain in silence with your eyes closed for a couple of minutes.

The idea is to listen and hear the voice of spirit from within, from without, from everywhere. The voice comes and heals. Keating says, "Contemplative Prayer is the opening of mind and heart - our whole being - to God, the Ultimate Mystery, beyond thoughts, words and emotions. We open our awareness to God whom we know by faith is within us, closer than breathing, closer than thinking, closer than choosing - closer than consciousness itself. Contemplative Prayer is a process of interior purification leading, if we consent, to divine union." As God speaks, the person realizes that he is loved and does not need to control and wage war. Centering prayer is a technique for peace, inner peace leading to outer peace. This technique is particularly helpful for the Caritas peacemaker because it leads to deep healing of feelings of control and security that lead to conflict. The deep feeling of being loved beyond personality is a basic way to heal yourself.

When you get in touch with the voice of spirit within, you know you are loved. We learned this from our research on how creativity heals. The Spirit Body Healing Study, conducted at University of Florida College of Nursing and Medicine, interviewed people who used creativity to heal. The participants had peak spiritual experiences in which they realized that they were loved. Whether by God, Goddesses, nature, or the earth, the patients in the study had spiritual experiences of realizing they were loved and were valued for who they were.

loving
Nurture - Feedback   Huddles - circle of   Nurture
Love - Nurture

Caritas is loving energy that embraces us to experience love. Being loved changes your world. When you feel loved, you can take criticism, you can learn from the one who loves you and from experience without being defensive. When you feel loved, you are not bothered by small annoying characteristics of a person or situation, you are tolerant and accepting. When you are loved, you see beauty, you feel love flowing through you to others. The love circles into you and back to the world. The experience of being loved and feeling love is the most powerful experience of life. It purifies us, heals us, and creates peace. Have you ever had the experience of being loved deeply by a lover or by God? Have you ever had the experience of loving another deeply, of falling in love? Do you remember how you felt towards the world when you were in love or being loved?

THOMAS KEATING ON PEACE AND SELF HEALING

"None of us can make a difference in the world, unless there is first a difference in us. This is what all the great spiritual teachers of the world's religious and spiritual traditions tell us – Jesus, Teresa of Avila, Lao Tze, Lord Krishna, the Buddha—and the great spiritual teachers today from the Dalai Lama to Mother Meera, to Sant Rajinder Singh, and many more say it time and time again--unless we start with ourselves, we will get nowhere in the world.

Nonviolence begins in the mind. Some people think that having violent thoughts is a good thing. It gets the violence out of our system. I have heard it said that "a thought murder a day keeps the psychotherapist away." That sounds cute, but the mystics warn us not to entertain a thought murder, thought assault, not even the thought of striking out verbally. The mystics tell us that even though thoughts are invisible to the eye, every thought takes on a subtle form, and every thought form sends out a vibration. If you walk into a room of people who are not speaking but only thinking hostile, angry thoughts, your first response may be, "I don't like the way it feels in here."

Our thought forms create palpable vibrations around us. And as far as I know, meditation is the only practice that gives us power over our own thoughts. If we do not learn to control the mind, the mind controls us. Someone walks in front of us in the store and cuts us off. The thought pops into the mind, "I'd like to break her legs. Or maybe, "That s.o.b. – who does he think he is?" The thought comes unbidden. Someone of a different ethnic group does or says something that we think is stupid and in our minds we say, "Figures, it's just like those people to do that."

How many hostile thoughts do we have in a day? Finding peace within begins by learning to control our thoughts – in the checkout line, while driving down the road, at work, at the dinner table – wherever we are, where we go, 24/7/365. Any thought that crosses the mind if when expressed or acted out would bring injury to another is a violent thought. Nonviolence is not about being passive or doing nothing. It is a way of life – a way of life that begins in our own minds because thoughts become words – words become deeds – deeds become habits – habits become a way of life – our way of life becomes character and character becomes our destiny.

And transformed individuals transform the families in which they live. Transformed individuals and families transform the communities in which they live. Transformed communities transform nations; transformed nations transform the world. We are all tied together in a garment of mutuality. When Jesus said, "Blessed are the Caritas peacemaker", he was reminding us that it is only when we change that the world around us really changes."

THE PATH TO INNER PEACE IS SAME PATH AS THE PATH TO OUTER PEACE...

As Keating eloquently says, the path to inner peace is same path as the path to outer peace. You need to know deeply who you are. You need to face your anger, hate, darkness, pain, hurt, and rage. You need to look directly at the face of rage, the face of pain, the face of anger, the face of your hatred in yourself. You need to see the many faces within the darkness, and then see the face of love, the face of gentle compassion. You need to see the multifaceted face that you are, see yourself in your wholeness, not just see one side without seeing the other.

The path to world peace is the path to inner peace. This is the same as the teachings of all religions. Look at yourself as you really are. Only when you see your own darkness and light, pain and joy, hatred and love, can you can start down the road to forgiveness. To experience hate, let it flow in silence without turning it on another- it is the teacher of love. The distance from your head with your thoughts and beliefs to your heart with your emotions and actions is huge. We all say we are for peace, and then we fight with our own husband, our own wife, our own brother, our own sister over the smallest thing. Healing yourself is moving from the head to the heart, from a belief in peace to real action for peace.

THE CARITAS ENERGETIC FIELD

The Caritas energetic field is a palpable vibrational energy that resides within our bodies and extends beyond our bodies. Hildegard Bingen described the same phenomenon when she said that the physical body resides in spirit. Imagine your body in its physical form residing within an energetic field of pure love that expands 5-8 feet beyond your body, holding you in a light of Caritas energy, your heart pulsating from an electric charge in rhythm with each heartbeat. Imagine this ray pumping the blood through your body, but then this energetic sense of a heart throb extends as a pulsation energetically through your physical being - your mind/emotions an energetic field expanding beyond your physical boundaries. This energetic field is a life force that has a wholeness, a uniqueness, an individualization - manifesting your life journey. This energy field has frequency rhythms, and when it interfaces with another human's field and the intention is love and caring, it enhances the fields while they come together to be even larger. The Caritas energetic field from one human being is capable of filling an entire room, as we have had experience with people who can do this. The energetic field is timeless spaciousness living within constructs of time and space. The energetic field is an essence connection to collective consciousness when groups are gathered together. The collective consciousness shared for world peace, nonviolence and love… the caritas energy field can be as large as a community, a nation, entire planet. As each human being intentionally becomes the light of Caritas, we become beacons of light and the world becomes enlightened.

Section Two

USING THE CARITAS TEN PROCESSES FOR PEACE

CHAPTER FOUR

CARITAS PROCESS 1. EXPERIENCING THE ENERGY OF LOVING KINDNESS

FEEL THE PEACEMAKING ENERGY OF LOVING KINDNESS.

Feeling loving kindness for yourself is necessary for peace. It is about embracing altruistic values and practicing loving kindness with yourself and others. It is the first step towards forgiveness and towards feeling love and compassion for others. In Buddhist meditation you go to a place where there is total compassion. You go to a place where you re-story your life from compassion and love. Become compassionate to yourself by seeing yourself from a distance, from the outside. Stand back and say, "Look at her. She needs ....." In a moment of witness, of reflection, see what you need to heal. When you see yourself with compassion, you can tend to your body as a sacred body, tend to emotions as natural forces that move through you. You can honor intuitions and insights, you can be illuminated to find your place in the world. When you feel the energy of love flowing through you, you will heal yourself and be able to become a Caritas peacemaker. When you feel compassion for yourself, the compassion will flow to others and peace will result.

 Compassion is a kind of love; it joins your light with another's. If you are ill, it joins you to a healer; if you are a healer, it joins you to the person you are healing; if you are making peace, it joins you to your enemy. When you are in compassion, you flow beyond your boundaries and merge with the person you are with. You see them without judgment, you see them with God's love. You see them as beautiful, as sacred, you see their spirit instead of their personality. God's love and compassion is natural, it is a feeling from the heart. It is not God telling you to seek vengeance.

The Caritas peacemaker who sees with compassion sees their enemy in a different way. If you are angry but can see those around you with compassion, you invite them to see you in this way too. Your love is felt by everyone and helps them love you with compassion too.

In compassion, you show your light. Compassion breaks the cycle of violence leading to more violence.

EXERCISES FOR FEELING LOVE

Imagine a light within you that is glowing. Imagine that when you are making peace, the light goes from you and merges with the light of the person you are with, and all of those around you. Imagine it magnifies and spreads around the whole earth.

To cultivate an experience of love, stop judgment. In your mind's eye, imagine your heart opening. Utilize a vibrational shift, shifting into deep breathing. Open again, be present. Move into a place inside yourself where you feel patience. Relax, allow time to become infinite. Listen to the story, focus on your own experience of awareness. Feel a surrender that has a vibrational quality. Everything slows down and you become quiet. There is a vibrational quality of the moment in becoming one with breath.

To feel the healing energy of love, first become aware of your body. Concentrate on sensations. Imagine your love, picture your lover or children or parents and then, relax and pay attention to feelings of buzzing, vibration, tingling, and numbness. When you feel the feelings, focus your mind on how they feel in your body, where they are most intense, what the actual sensation is. Do it over and over again until you know what the feeling of relaxation is in your body.

Pay attention to your body as you have your own experience of going deeper into embodying spirit. Notice feelings of tingling and buzzing you have that accompany your spiritual visions of God or angels and peak experiences of connectedness and oneness.

As the peak experience comes to you, notice what happens as it approaches. Many people glimpse it in advance, and when they see it coming, their body feels different from usual.

Notice feelings of purification or cleansing. Be aware of how the energy seems to fill you up. Notice changes in your breathing.

Then see If the feelings of the energy of love seem to be followed by deep feelings of being at peace.

CREATING A CARITAS ENERGETIC FIELD

The steps in creating a Caritas Energetic Field are centering on our heart and beginning to cultivate a direct relationship through our heart center to the infinite field of cosmic love.

As you stand on the earth, your feet are grounded with an intimate connection to earth energies. This earth energy is tangible, physical, and felt. It comes through the connection that spirals up from the earth, and connects at the heart center, intersecting the earth energy and a comic universal energy from above. The human being intersects the energy of love and the earth energy. The human resides within a spiritual Universal energetic field. The earth energy comes up, the love energy comes down, and they intersect in your heart. A human lives within a universal consciousness.

You can fill your energy body with light and the earth energy that intersects at your heart. This is based on an expanded view of the human being where the human energy field is capable of opening up and connecting to a source. The source can be defined as one's relationships with the divine spirit or God. The heart connected with the source has the ability to become expansive and healing. It is coherent, it is connected with the ray of one's own heart and the pulsation of the Universe, and the rhythm of the earth. It is a practice of interconnectedness with the sacred body as it is a manifestation of the earth. The sacred body has the capacity to be a vortex with energy frequencies that radiate vibration. Intention allows us to transform this earth energy by bringing in a feeling state that can be cultivated of love and peace. Love and peace are states of authentic self realization.

For example, remember a moment of joy and gratitude. Allow this feeling state to fill your heart, focusing your attention on your heart, breathing deeply, feeling the rhythm of your breath deepening, and listening, and seeing into your own heart center. Breathe in allow your breathing to slow down, allow the heart feeling to expand your feelings of gratitude and appreciation. Create a positive feeling state as if it was happening right now. Allow this feeling state to extend beyond the heart center to expand the energetic state throughout the entire body. Expand it to others and to 5-8 inches around your body, imagining your heart's electromagnet field in light energy as a slowly expanding matrix of light energy radiating in concentric circles around your heart and body. This experience is your connection, your belonging to the galaxy and Universal light matrix that has a heartbeat of its own. In this pleasant moment experience no time/ timelessness, no form/ spaciousness - experience yourself as a vast openness, a vortex of energy. Transform this energy into love. Love is eternal.

EXERCISE TO HAVE COMPASSION FOR YOURSELF

Feeling compassion for yourself, seeing yourself without judgment, takes practice. We have all been trained for a lifetime in self criticism and self judgment. We are all very judgmental of ourselves, and it is hard to release the eye of the inner critic. We learned this from parents, school and church.

You can change your view of yourself to someone who can see yourself with compassion, to someone who is compassionate. Here is an exercise to increase your feelings of compassion. Begin by seeing out of eyes of the Buddha, of Mother Teresa or the most compassionate person you can think of. Look out of their eyes at yourself. That exercise is a practice called *The Buddha of Compassion*. Let the deity or compassionate person you choose gaze at you with compassionate eyes and see you completely with love. Let them see you inside and outside. Just letting yourself be seen compassionately is an enormous thing.

After you let yourself be seen compassionately by a compassionate one, imagine them entering your body and filling you up to your very capacity, to the very edges of your skin, and see the world through their eyes. See through the eyes of compassion. As you do this, you are yourself but you're also seeing through the eyes of compassion. If you are basically a judgmental person, or you have expectations,

Nursing staff + Uniqueness
Beauty

give yourself over to the one who fills you and gives you the ability
to have compassion. When you are present with another person and
see them without judgment, with love and acceptance, what you see
is their beauty and their uniqueness.

Now use the exercise to feel compassion for your enemy. See your
enemy through the eyes of the compassionate one. Let their eyes replace yours for a moment. See the person's beauty. See them love
their family. See their love of their country and its people and their religious beliefs. See their childhood and hurts and suffering. Feel their
point of view towards you and your position. Now let all that go and
feel love and compassion through the eyes of the compassionate one
for your enemy.

The practice of the Buddha of compassion can help you increase your
ability to be compassion to yourself and others. If your grandmother
is the most compassionate person that you have ever known, imagine that you are sitting across from your grandmother, and she is
looking at you with total love and acceptance. Just sit there and be
with them; allow yourself to be seen and ask them to help you not be
judgmental of yourself as you heal with spirit.

A GUIDED IMAGERY TO EXPERIENCE COMPASSION

See yourself sitting in your home in a place that is comfortable. Picture
the most compassionate person you can imagine sitting across from
you. It can be a person you know, a loved one, a family member,
a religious figure, a teacher, a presence from nature. Picture them
looking at you, right into your eyes as deeply as imaginable. Let them
look right into your soul, past your personality. Let them see you in
your most beautiful aspect, as the most loving person you can be.
They can do this, that is why you have chosen them to come. Let that
feeling of being seen with compassion come over you completely.
Absorb the way it feels to be loved without limits, without conditions.
Feel the universal love come over you.

Now go into their body and look out of their eyes. Imagine you can see yourself the way you were just seen. See yourself as endlessly beautiful, as perfectly loving, as the way you are beyond your personality. See yourself the way you are seen by Jesus, by Great Spirit, by the Blessed Mother. Now look out of their eyes to your enemy. See they way they are seen by Jesus, Great Spirit, by the Blessed Mother.

Now realize you are that compassionate person. You can have compassion for yourself and your enemy the way they have compassion for you. Only by embodying the spirit of compassion and love will there be world peace. The work is inner work, consciousness work; hard, wonderful work.

A GUIDED IMAGERY TO EXPERIENCE SELF LOVE

Make yourself comfortable. You can be sitting down or lying down. Loosen tight clothing, uncross your legs and arms. Close your eyes. Let your breathing slow down. Take several deep breaths. Let your abdomen rise as you breathe in, and fall as you let your deep breath out. As you breathe in and out you will become more and more relaxed. You may feel feelings of tingling, buzzing, or relaxation; if you do, let those feelings increase. You may feel heaviness or lightness, you may feel your boundaries loosening and your edges softening.

Now let yourself relax. Let your feet relax, let your legs relax. Let the feelings of relaxation spread upwards to your thighs and pelvis. Let your pelvis open and relax. Now let your abdomen relax, let your belly expand, do not hold it in anymore. Now let your chest relax, let your heartbeat and breathing take place by themselves. Let your arms relax, your hands relax. Now let your neck relax, your head, your face. Let your eyes relax, see a horizon and blackness for a moment. Let these feelings of relaxation spread throughout your body. Let your relaxation deepen. If you wish you can count your breaths and let your relaxation deepen with each breath.

In your mind's eye picture yourself as the Caritas peacemaker. Then, in your mind's eye, go to a place in the center of your body. It can be your belly, your heart, your spine. In your center is a light. It is a flickering light, it is soft like a candle flame. Now in your imagination see this light glowing brighter and brighter. See the sphere of light expand. Feel this light expand around your fingers, feel it expand down to your toes. Feel this soft, warm, translucent, golden light surround you and embrace you. Now in your imagination feel the light expanding around your body, see the glowing light growing, see your entire body glowing. See the light move beyond the boundaries of your skin, see it expand around you from one foot to two feet away. Feel the light swirling gently, moving. It has a beauty, an ebb and flow; it is soft, it has a rhythm that pulsates like your heart.

Now imagine that this light becomes transformed into the energy of love. Your body is immersed in the glow of living light and you are being healed, cleansed, you are being loved. The source of this love is a pulsation from within you. Now imagine that this light, this love and this energy are you. Now in your mind's eye, expand this light to about four feet around you. Now it is interfaced, merged with the light from others around you. You are interconnected and your love blends with those around you. The light brightens as it interfaces, it becomes magnified in its intensity and flows out of your body. It is spinning, soft, beautiful. Your love is spinning around your own body and the other. You are in a relationship, it is easy, you are in grace and total peace. All you have to do is breathe. Now let the light fill the whole room, then the house, then the city, then the country, then the country of your enemy, then the earth, then the solar system, then the galaxy, then the universe.

When you are ready, return to the room where you are doing the exercise. First move your feet and then move your hands. Move them around and experience the feeling of the movement. Press your feet down onto the floor, feel the grounding, feel the pressure on the bottom of your feet, feel the solidity of the earth. Feel your backside on the chair; feel your weight pressing downwards. Now open your eyes. Look around you. Stand up and stretch, move your body, feel it move.

You are back; you can carry the experience of the exercise outward to your life. You will feel stronger and be able to see deeper. You will be in a healing state. Each time you do the exercise you will be more relaxed and be able to go deeper and be more powerful as a Caritas peacemaker.

CHAPTER FIVE

CARITAS PROCESS 2. USING AUTHENTIC PRESENCE FOR PEACE

In Caritas, authentic presence is a way of being and an action. It is about faith and hope and honoring others. Integrity, presence, intent and commitment are states of mind that make the way of being actual and empower your actions. You can greatly increase your ability to live in peace by using these tools. Peace work is inner work projected outwards. Intention and commitment give us focused ways of increasing our resolve and motivation. They clarify our purpose and make us decisive in our actions.

THE LAW OF INTEGRITY

You can increase your ability to live in peace by using personal integrity. Your ability to live in peace comes from your authenticity as a human being. That is why a Caritas peacemaker has a deep commitment to integrity. The Caritas peacemaker is honest about the presentation of who she or he is. People of peace are honest in their intention to be in support of the people around them and they honor people and support them for who they are. They listen to a person and see clearly what they do. They honor the integrity of a person's actions and respect people for their diversity.

Integrity comes from a core strength within, it comes from your core essence. Your physical world vibrates with the essence of who you are. What you are in the external world vibrates and resonates from your internal world, your essence within. If you stripped yourself down to your essence and built upon that, each step would create yourself in integrity. Each feeling, each article of clothing, each authentic act would be an expression of your essence. You would be true to your inner form, authentic and honest.

Integrity is a commitment to yourself, it is being who you are in your essence. For women to be who they are, they need to take off the cloaks and veils that surround them. They need to drop their conceptual framework, their political parties, their husband's perspective. They need to strip down to what they are, what they are inside as Caritas peacemakers for Peace. For men to be who they are, they

62

Nursing—drop Medical's perpective.
Own perspective

need to take off the costumes they wear, the ties and suits of corporate culture. They need to drop their work identity, their political parties, their propped up persona created to impress women. They need to strip down to what they are, what they are inside as Caritas peacemakers for Peace.

AUTHENTIC PRESENCE

Authentic Presence lets you be one with the person you are in conflict with. It is a powerful tool for peace. To be an effective Caritas peacemaker you need to be present in the here and now. To be totally present you need to shift away from the ordinary talking in your mind. Pause, slow down, stop your mind chatter. Put aside your daily concerns such as who picks up your child, or dealing with your car repair bills. Put aside the things that are distracting your attention. Breathe, pause, put concerns aside and deliberately do not focus on them. You can deal with them later but be present with yourself first.

To be present in the moment, slow down your breathing, be consciousness of your body. Feel yourself in the moment. Look around you and notice shapes, shadows, color, and textures- notice all the things around you. Feel the temperature; allow your eyes to become open to colors. Feel how saturated and differentiated the colors are.

To use presence as a Caritas peacemaker, face the individual you are working with to make peace. Look at their face; look into their eyes. Look at them as if it is what your life is about in that moment. You are in a moment of communion with them; part of being with them is seeing them. See color of their hair, their eyes, their skin. Watch their gestures. Allow yourself to be empty, allow them to fill you up. Use your sense of smell, touch, and sight. See the face unveiling its essence to you. The unveiling of their face has to do with the unveiling of your face. You become accessible to yourself at the moment you allow the other to come forward. Presence means they are inside your own body. Silence allows them to fill with their life, voice,

Caritas Sisters

Huddles- moment of communion

Village →Circle of Caritas

thoughts. Using presence in this way eliminates separateness, make you one, stops the me verses you.

Experience the fullness of your own energy. Become empty of your own self-absorbed concerns. Be consciousness of what you are as a Caritas peacemaker… you fill from within, you radiate your energy and attention outwards. Your fullness is felt as your presence. You cultivate your fullness through practice. It comes through your eyes, your voice, your touch. Wait for them to fill you, then move forward from what they have given you.

Use your breath. Breath fills you up. Expand on the fullness of your breath. Come from a place of pure light. Energy has a resonance, it reverberates with soft subtle vibrations.

Feel it, it is the life force- chi, prana. This energy is what you use for healing and making peace. This energy is what you feel in your own life when you vibrate with the life force. One way to be present is to connect your self, to be in alignment with, the force of your own life.

You feel this as inner light, as your life force energy. You are the conduit for spirit energy, God's energy, to move through you. When you make peace with spirit energy you are not depleted; the energy enhances you, connects you to the life force. When you get in alignment with the energy from above, you are revitalized as you make peace. Tap into energy in alignment with God's light on earth, with forces that are positive. You are in sublime balance of energy, the energy moves through you so you are not depleted. Try this with your husband, wife or lover, with your children or parents, with your associates and finally, when you can do that, with your enemy.

ACTIVITIES AND EXERCISES TO BECOME PRESENT

- Practice being present with people wherever you are.
- Look and watch people closely.
- Hold them in your psychic space.

- Observe, don't be distracted from them as humans.
- Make meaningful conversation.
- Care about them
- Recognize yourself in another.
- Mirror, see the refection of your own soul in the other.

See spirit within yourself and in others, make meaning, create connections. Remember, we are all one. Clean up the smoky mirror of prejudice and make it the clear vision of love. When you are present with your enemy- you see them as yourself through the eyes of God.

OBSTACLES TO PRESENCE FOR PEACE

- Triggers about your own beliefs being right
- Defensiveness and fear
- Holding back from telling what you think
- Holding back from being your authentic self
- Seeing differences, not similarities
- Not identifying feelings of "you and they" that keep you apart
- Feeling separation
- Triggering your paranoid thoughts
- Not believing
- Feeling grossed out
- Remembering family issues and feuds
- Racial prejudice
- Being stuck in the past wars
- Thinking, "they are evil, I am good."
- Religious prejudice
- Material greed

THE ZEN OF SEEING WITH LOVE

- Slow your eyes down. —Pause
- Feel and caress the textures of what you are seeing.
- See colors, shadow, and light.
- Hear sounds, tones, silence, and pulsations
- Touch, move to allow the other to be embraced.
- Imagine: "I Embrace you with my attention."
- See them with love and let your love be seen.

Patients, staff stakeholders

PEACEMAKING IS BEING NESS,

Peacemaking is being ness. Peacemaking is being in a path less traveled, the path of walking in new shoes. Peacemaking is the expanding consciousness of both people touching. It is about being with another, about two people, just being. As the Caritas peacemaker creates a sacred place when someone comes to them, there is a pattern of being manifesting as energy, a resonating energy of the intention of making peace.

Look at what we take for granted in the environment we are working in. Take from granted, look at someone's face as if you have never seen a face, see the baby out of the mother's eyes. Peacemaking is about ways of being… examine your ways of being. It is about waking up to what people are asking for. When a person is with a Caritas peacemaker, deep in their soul, they want a communion of being ness.

Rumi, the Middle Eastern poet said:

"Out beyond ideas of wrongdoing and right doing, there is a field.

I will meet you there."

A GUIDED IMAGERY TO BE PRESENT

Make yourself comfortable. You can be sitting down or lying down. Loosen tight clothing, uncross your legs and arms. Close your eyes. Let your breathing slow down. Take several deep breaths. Let your abdomen rise as you breathe in, and fall as you let your deep breath out. As you breathe in and out you will become more and more relaxed. You may feel feelings of tingling, buzzing, or relaxation… if you do, let those feelings increase. You may feel heaviness or lightness, you may feel your boundaries loosening and your edges softening.

Now let yourself relax. Let your feet relax, let your legs relax. Let the feelings of relaxation spread upwards to your thighs and pelvis. Let your pelvis open and relax. Now let your abdomen relax, let your belly expand, do not hold it in anymore. Now let your chest relax, let your heartbeat and breathing take place by themselves. Let your arms relax, your hands relax. Now let your neck relax, your head, your face. Let your eyes relax, see a horizon and blackness for a moment. Let these feelings of relaxation spread throughout your body. Let your relaxation deepen. If you wish you can count your breaths and let your relaxation deepen with each breath.

Now, in your mind's eye let yourself be in a situation where you are making peace. It can be your own home or relative's home with a family member in conflict… a workplace, a peace march, a place with an adversary. Picture the scene in detail… feel it, see it, hear it, smell it, touch it. Let the intensity of the scene fill you and take you. Now as you are there, simply be there. Be aware of your thoughts and when they roam bring them back gently to the place you are in. Say to yourself over and over again, I am where I am, I am present here, only here.

Now look very closely at exact detail. Look at the details as if they are your reason for living. Pay attention to them as if they could jump at you and eat you; be alert. Pay attention to them so you see anything move, anything change shape or color. Look like you are looking for the slightest movement or change to come. Go deeper now, look for feelings in you that are triggered by what you see-- memories, images, visions-- and then come back and look again. It is as if you are on a river… your mind wanders, the river calls you back; be on the river, that is where you are, you can't see anything here if you are not here. So in the scene you are picturing: be on it, in it, see it, you can't see anything there if you are somewhere else.

When you are ready, return to the room where you are doing the exercise. First move your feet and then move your hands. Move them around and experience the feeling of the movement. Press your feet down onto the floor, feel the grounding, feel the pressure on the bottom of your feet, feel the solidity of the earth. Feel your backside on the chair; feel your weight pressing downwards. Now open your eyes. Look around you. Stand up and stretch, move your body, feel it move. You are back; you can carry the experience of the exercise outward to your life. You will feel stronger and be able to see deeper. You will be in a peaceful state. Each time you do the exercise you will be more relaxed and be able to go deeper and be more effective as a Caritas peacemaker.

INTENTION IS CULTIVATED

Intention gives you power as a Caritas peacemaker and helps you hone your skills. Your intention to be a Caritas peacemaker comes from a process you cultivate over years. When you have clear intention, your training, education and learning become fine tuned. Your intentions take your mastery and activate your own skills. You are faced with a war and you need to decide what to do to make peace. In the event, what acts on the moment is all your preparation, all the skill building you have been through. The point of contact is then instrumental; in that moment you are focused on one specific outcome.

Intention allows for openness, sincerity, and compassion. Intention is integral in all steps of peacemaking. There is intention to create sacred space, intention to solve the problem at hand that is creating the environment for war, intention to be present. There is intention to do each thing, to see and understand. There is intention to be a Caritas peacemaker, intention to change the world. Intention is the undercurrent of all you do in the process of living.

There is a practice that cultivates the power of your intention. Intention is amplified by practice. What are your skills? Expand the possibility of your skills, go further; expand the parameters you are comfortable with. Look for new experiences and deeper understandings and embody them in your own work. Within intent, you grow.

Explore – grow

Your skills are a vessel. They anchor your whole life with the peacemaking process you are working on. The image of intent sparks the engine to do the work. Intent is the fire within pushing you forward to your goal. What fuels your own fire, what fuels your own passion? You harness the fire within you to drive your own intention to be a Caritas peacemaker.

Intention of the moment

If your intention is to be powerful, your power grows; if your intention is to be compassionate, you fill with compassion. Intent fuels your momentum; inside intention is your momentum. Intent is volition pushing you forward to your target or goal. The archer practices to hit the target. Intention is the arrow going forward. But here… it is an arrow to peace.

The Caritas peacemakers for Peace's intent is also based on their image of themselves. If you have faith in the possibility of peace and problem resolution, if you believe in the paradigm of peace, your intent grows. If you believe you're the one who can do it, intent grows. Have faith and confidence in the process, believe in your own power to make peace and your ability to call it forth, believe in your intention to empower everyone to hold a new consensus of peace as the usual state of the world.

PRACTICE USING AUTHENTIC PRESENCE AND INTENTION FOR PEACE

- Define your intention clearly, write it down.
- List your goals for peace clearly.
- List your skills to promote the goal.
- Constantly be in the process of learning and yearning for more.
- Lean forwards to who you will become and what you are learning.
- Join your mastery with creativity.
- Involve your belief system; whatever story you hold for peace defines your specific intention.

OBSTACLES TO INTENT FOR PEACE:

- Over stimulation and scattering your work
- Being distracted by not being clear about what you have to do
- Floating without defining what you are doing
- Over-commitment and unrealistic goals
- Rushing and poor time management
- Exhaustion and burn-out
- Conflict of appointments or interests
- Petty arguments over details✓
- Prejudice and defensiveness
- Taking conflict in or out of the peace movement personally

A GUIDED IMAGERY FOR INCREASING YOUR AUTHENTIC PRESENCE

Begin with your usual preparation for meditation, as described before, going through the process until you have reached that deep place of relaxation and receptivity.

Be present
— home — work

Now in your mind's eye picture yourself as the Caritas peacemaker you are. See yourself, the place and the work you are doing. It can be your own home or a relative's home with a family member in conflict, a workplace, a peace march, a place with an adversary. See it, hear it, smell it, feel it, touch it. Be there deeply. Now pause a moment, remember who you are, remember your skills, your abilities… the time you have spent preparing to be in the place you are now. Now concentrate on your intent to make peace. Focus it, sharpen it. Like holding a bow and aiming at a target, set your goal as a healer and aim it precisely at the target. Clarify what you are doing and now put fire and energy behind this intent. Take a breath, and power your intent deeply with all the energy that you have. Go inwards to your inner voices and hear them power your intent, hear your guides and teachers power your intent to heal. Picture a fire within you that grows and makes your intent more powerful. In your mind's eye picture your intent as a line leading from you to the world for peace.

Now take the intent and your personal power and commit to it. In your mind's eye say to yourself, I am committed to being a Caritas peacemaker and creating peace. I will give everything I have to be the Caritas peacemaker I am. Think of an offering you will give for your intent. Let it come to you, now give it to the earth in a promise to commit to peace work with full intent, to commit to that moment with all the intent that you have. If you wish, you can ask yourself how committed you are to doing this work. What would you give to do this, to create peace?. If you have worked for years as a Caritas peacemaker, the answer is true. You have been and are giving a great part of your life to be the Caritas peacemaker you are. Now give this with intent, consciously, as a decision. I will give my fullest intent in this moment to create world peace and to be the vehicle and facilitator of the peace in the moment. I do.

When you are ready, return to the room where you are doing the exercise. First move your feet and then move your hands. Move them around and experience the feeling of the movement. Press your feet down onto the floor, feel the grounding, feel the pressure on the bottom of your feet, feel the solidity of the earth. Feel your backside on the chair; feel your weight pressing downwards. Now open your eyes. Look around you. Stand up and stretch, move your body, feel it move. You are back; you can carry the experience of the exercise outward to your life. You will feel stronger and be able to see deeper. You will be in a healing state. Each time you do the exercise you will be more relaxed and be able to go deeper and be more deeply healed.

COMMITMENT TO PEACE

When you make a commitment to your own path as a Caritas peacemaker, that commitment reminds you how to act. You constantly deal with choice, each choice leads you to work for peace. Each choice is another step to being in union with your higher self. A choice which honors your body, honors your life, honors suffering, honors pain, is your choice for life. We have come to a time when those who are Caritas peacemakers for Peace stand apart from those who are not. We have come to a time when those who are Caritas peacemakers for Peace act differently from those who are not.

You need commitment to be a Caritas peacemaker when you come to the point where you know you are different. People may not want you to take that path, it may be unpopular. What is difficult is having commitment when people around you have commitment to the other way. Commitment to the way of peace is often unpopular. When millions march for peace, it becomes much easier. You say to yourself, how can you not see it my way, how can you be that way?

How can you make a commitment based on faith and belief? People have done it forever. How do people commit to faith? What is the human phenomenon of faith? In commitment, we create the future. Right now is different from any other time. There is an awareness factor. Inside of this crisis is a beginning of great things to come. People who understand have an opportunity to direct people. People are paying attention, looking at their life, examine what is important and not. We all have a part in sharing

Leadership - Commited to faith and belief.

what we know so others can see it, hear it. Having knowledge is an opportunity to share what we know.

— opportunities

There are many stories in this crisis about the doorway for change, about the opportunity that we have now for a positive future. A crisis is a time to let go of karma, an opportunity for clarity, an opening. It is a spiritual time to create a new reality. It is brand new, it is a doorway that never occurred in this way before. We created the doorway through our communication with each other and our feelings of oneness and peace. The doorway comes from the energy we have all put into visionary, spiritual and inner growth work for the last years, the doorway to recreate everything. Commitment is the incredible power we feel in our work moving forward; it is the urgency we feel in the balance between peace and war.

Communication - doorway
Huddles - Feeling of oneness and peace

COMMITMENT HAS BEEN AWAKENED BY 9/11 AND THE WAR

A painter wrote this:

"When I saw 9/11, I felt my commitment strengthen. I felt shock- and then felt a wall torn in the world, a cluster of souls taken, a sacrifice to illuminate something. I knew I had to have the ability to see what was illuminated. The challenge was based on my own ability to see and be awake. Commitment holds true to what you have understood about the world, it holds true in the moment.

Stand tall, love someone, see the world with no war. Believe in infinite choices and possibilities. You in your simple way can make a difference by just being committed to yourself and your own actions- knowing they will make a huge difference in the world. It

starts with you being committed to peace in your own life. Look where in your own life you cause pain, access that hurt, and heal it. That heal yourself and the other. Start with your most intimate relationship, move outwards to your enemy. It is time.

I had to learn from the pain, anger, and suffering in my own life. I had to look at my most intimate relationships-- was I in these relationships with peace? If not, what could I do differently. This is an opportunity to change, to be more committed. I had to look closely at what I thought I could not do. Now I do not have any choice not to do it- an event in the external world has stunned me.

In this crisis, I felt and saw the two paths. I stopped in the road and I clearly realized there were two paths going in two different directions. I had come to a fork in the road of my own life and I had to make a choice. These choices in life don't come easy, they are a time to let go of burdens. I felt like everything would be taken away. I thought, it is time to let go of things, if we will die and time goes by so swiftly, how can my life make a difference? When I strive for peace, commit to peace, I commit myself to a moment of silence, to rest, calm, fasting, to protecting living things, to the wind, trees, earth, flowers, and species. I become connected to the interface of life."

If you were the enlightened one, if she and he were no one else but you, and you were asked to give what you have to share in this important moment- what would you say?

Commitment is a simple act. You feel it resonating within your body like an essential vibrating energy. You hold to as deeply as your breath and know it is an essential truth to you in this world, in this lifetime. It has come to you as an essential part of life, a feeling, a certainty.

Your Commitment is to Yourself and God

A Native Americans friend told me, "To make a commitment is to endure suffering". Many Native American groups do a four day vision quest, without food and water, to make a commitment more real and powerful. These people do this for healing and peace. They say that their commitment is a sacrifice, a gift to their people. They say that when you make a commitment, you sacrifice something and the world will change; hold the commitment, you do your best in every

benefits
Sacrifice - Nursing

moment. There is no judgment, no right and wrong; you do what is best from your experience.

the circle - share experiences

To make a commitment, start with a prayer. Make God or the Creator part of it. Get help from the spirits, ancestors, and God in being successful in the commitment. It is not trivial, it is difficult. Difficulties can makes the commitment come to you even more powerfully. Don't be afraid; you commit with your whole life. You cannot help it. You make the commitment to a higher force, it is a personal promise, it is not to other people. It is to yourself. You ask for help, you have other people pray for you. It is a powerful urge and goal to make the commitment.

Finally you believe the commitment will change the world. You are powerful, your actions contribute to changing the world. Your action matters. Your prayers make the sun rise. The Caritas peacemakers for Peace were always people who healed the earth.

CHAPTER SIX

CARITAS PROCESS 3. SPIRITUALITY, HEALING YOUR OWN LIFE

An important part of becoming a more effective Caritas peacemaker is spirituality, healing your own life. It is about being sensitive to self and others by nurturing individual beliefs and practices. It helps dealing with fear and blockages, with anger and hate, with resistance and personal issues. The Caritas peacemaker way of being is a lived experience, not a theory. It goes right to a person's early childhood experiences. The Caritas peacemaker is up against their most personal issues of ego, anger, faith, evil, confidence, trust, power, and purpose. Being a Caritas peacemaker is about being who you are, and that is challenging for anyone. Our teaching is to start by healing your own defensiveness and attachments to being right... to go out in nature, meditate, and learn to hear your own voices of wisdom within. Heal your own life by seeing who you really are and learning to love and accept yourself and others.

HEALING YOURSELF

One of first steps in becoming a Caritas peacemaker is to heal yourself. You can only do peacemaking from a place that is clear. It is necessary to clear the body, mind, and spirit of personal issues that trigger anger and defensiveness- this means healing yourself.

Healing yourself is an ongoing process that deepens and enriches your ability to be connected to others and be powerful as a Caritas peacemaker. Healing yourself has to do with allowing your essence to be expressed and seen. To do this, focus on what your spirit needs so you can move beyond your personality, so you can become larger than your own present life. When you are clear about your own issues, you can function in relationships with others in an open way. In a relationship with someone else, you need to be able to rescind your own needs, to drop judgments, opinions, and personal idiosyncrasies. Being a Caritas peacemaker is not about who you are and what you want, it is about what the situation you are working with is, and what it needs for a peaceful solution. ⟨ Conflict Resolution.

The way you heal is to experience transcendence. You experience your own ability to have altered states and be large. With the experience of transcendence in an altered state, you become larger than yourself. You have a spiritual connection with God. It is like being a Bodhisattva, like being enlightened. You function from a higher way of being with God, of God, interconnected with God. Everything you do is in communion with God. Everything you do is with total compassion, total love, the wisdom of the Bodhisattva. Heal yourself inside your work as a Caritas peacemaker. This spiritual sense of connectedness and oneness is not about being better than another, being right, or fighting a war for religion. All humans are one spirit; peace and love are pure spiritual concepts.

THE JOURNEY FROM HEAD TO HEART

Most people think one thing and feel and do another. We have an idealized way of thinking about ourselves and our beliefs- but the actions in our lives often come from anger, hurt, fear, or pain. We may believe in our mind that we are not prejudiced, we may believe we are fair and just, we may believe in freedom and liberty, we may believe we are all brothers and sisters, we may believe we honor each human being; but at the same time, we unwillingly and unknowing hurt people around us by our actions and words. It is time to examine the way we live and the way we impact other people. It is time for a close examination, a self examination, to see what we project and believe about other people. It is necessary to become clear about those projections and where the sources of the projections are.

The source of all thoughts, feelings, and actions stem from our own life- from us. When we accept full responsibility for our own lives, for our pain and happiness, we can accept our own power to change ourselves and the world. The road from head to heart is the journey of our lifetime. To move from what we want to believe and what is true about ourselves is a long and difficult process. We may think something in the outside world is causing us problems. Apparently, someone causes us to react, but inside our life we have choices- to stay or move away, to react in a different way. Our own ability to realize who we are is powerful- it is important that we understand that we help create our own lives.

The first step on the journey from head to heart is to realize the world has its short comings. All people have problems; in many instances people make their own lives difficult. They help make their own sorrow, suffering, and pain. To accept the imperfections of life is essential in being able to move forward and heal the world's suffering.

Second, become clear that your own problems and shortcomings cause your own suffering. Your ability to heal others is in essence dependent on your ability to heal yourself. In healing your own life, you cultivate wisdom and the ability to understand and experience others. In this process it is important to wake up to ourselves, to wake up to our own reactions, to wake up to our own perpetual patterns of being. It is necessary to become conscious of the way we create reactions in others. It is important to be aware of our thoughts that have the power of physical manifestation in the world. It is important to become awake to our own gestures, the tone of our voice, our movements through space and time... to be aware of the ripple effect on others of our presence in the world.

Our experience of defensiveness, our reactions of anger, our holding on to opinions all emerge in the context of relationships. When we immediately react to a person as if they are doing something to us, we are trapped in a reaction of pain and suffering and create conflict. In the moment of the defensive reaction, there is a pause and a time for a reflective stance. We need to examine what we see in the situation that is difficult. We need to cultivate a place of detachment and let the person be who they are. We need to realize it is our experience that causes the defensiveness, even though we think the other person is the problem. When we are angered by someone's aggression- we become aggressive. In that moment, we have to take the opportunity to understand our own aggression.

This is an important step for the Caritas peacemaker. It is crucial to understanding the experience of the other person who is being aggressive to us.

A big step in making peace is accepting people for who they are. The most important thing in tolerance is to allow people to have full expression of who they are. To experience the fullness of another human being- let go of control and expectations of them being who you want them to be, being someone different..

X Conflict Resolution.

A crisis is an opportunity for transformation. Open yourself up to a posture of learning. Take full responsibly for your own life beliefs and circumstances, and your ability to create a world where people are tolerated and accepted. This is a difficult meditation, it is not easy. Our natural tendency is to hold on to our own habits; instead, be aware of our own inadequacy, arrogance, and short comings. Claim them, own them, do something about them in any moment they appear.

Love Yourself = Accept Yourself

Third, loving yourself has to do with giving yourself permission to have the inadequacies and shortcomings that are yours. This self acceptance expands your ability to let others have shortcomings. Your ability to understand yourself clearly is related to your ability to understand others. This requires detachment- literally letting go- and allowing people the integrity of their own wholeness.

Defensiveness has to do with protecting yourself from the admission of your own inability to be open and tolerant with other individuals. It has to do with defensiveness of holding on to being right- which becomes more important than making peace. It blocks learning and openness. It stops dialogue and creates instant conflict.

In relationships, it is important to be clear about when you want to create peace in a situation. If peace is the goal, it is of the utmost importance to accept your own faults, your own participation in creating the conflict. Your power as a Caritas peacemaker lies in your own ability to have a choice of your own actions. You need to know that you have the ability to influence circumstances to move towards peace.

You can influence peace in any situation even if it's an unseen result. You can't do that if you are trapped in defensiveness, anger, and fear.

Try this with your closest relationships… your husband, wife, lover, children, parents, grandparents, friends, associates, and then.. your adversaries.

UNDERSTAND CARITAS PEACE, THE STEPS TO STOPPING DEFENSIVENESS BY UNDERSTANDING AND LOVING YOURSELF

- Realize the world has shortcomings but your reactions to them are yours.
- Don't blame others for your anger and defensiveness- the emotions are yours.
- Release the other as the cause of your anger and defensiveness.
- Understand that your own shortcomings are what cause your own emotions.
- Understand your role in conflict- what do you do to cause others to react to you.
- Accept your own shortcomings- you are human conditioned by culture.
- Do what you can to change if you want peace.
- Love yourself as beautiful.
- Love others as beautiful.

INSIDE THE MEMBRANE IS THE JOINING.

Inside the minds of every woman and every man is a place between reality and the visionary world. There is a shimmering membrane, a sliver that we can slip into. There, in a mystical space, each woman and each man can reach out and take the hand of the other. Inside that membrane of love we say, "I see you, I honor you, and I love you." That act is crucial to being a human. If every woman and man can enact that moment with a person they see each day, she or he finds there is a presence there who comes to her or him and speaks from within the membrane.

The presence is the Goddess and the God; it is She who gardens us from above, the feminine spiritual force, it is He who plants the seed, the masculine spiritual force. This force will take her or his hand and lead us forward. From the mystical place within each woman and each man we find that we are not alone. Who is She, who is He, an angel? I feel like it is God, the sacred part of each one of us. God reflects this spirit for the woman, for the man. What is the spirit like? It is anonymous, it is like light, it has a form which cannot be defined; it is infinite, immeasurable, it is fluid, it flows like a river, it feels watery. It is all women and all men, it is one woman and one man. She is all expressions of women and men. She is deep love to be given to you. He is deep love to be given to you. From within yourself, know you are loved.

THE BODY FAMILIAR

Being familiar with your own body is basic to understanding life. This is what being alive is about. It is about holding something in its death, birth, pain, and knowing the depth of its life inside your own body. It is not empathy, it is a depth of connection and knowing that is embodied.

When you fall in love, there is an intimacy of knowing another's soul, of touching their soul and reaching out as an act of love. It is being friends before you are friends. It is seeing someone's beauty or breath. It can happen with ordinary people; you look into someone's eyes and see a beautiful person. If you wanted to fall in love- you could fall in love in that moment. It is intimacy.

Women can fall into the wonderful experience of caring or being cared for. Women can do this in a moment,,, a nurse can care for a patient, a mother can care for a child. That is the power of woman.

The connection happens by giving and receiving. The man can learn from this natural nurturing and caring. This caring is the opposite of war. The body familiar is the doorway to nurturing and peace.

USE YOUR BODY AS A VORTEX TO HEALING.

Use your body to listen and see, to learn about peace, inside and outside. This learning needs to come from a clarity within you that is your essence. If you are in a process that allows negativity to release, you become clearer and clearer. You need to flow like a river, to see yourself moving. There are three steps to healing yourself for peace:

1. Create a process that allows you to take notice of your own negative stuff, of your own dysfunctional patterns of fighting and anger. Make a commitment to heal yourself and your anger with therapy, body work, exercise, fitness, diet change, cleansing.

2. Look at your own life, assess your personal and individual needs for change, and create a process that is intentionally healing of your anger for yourself for peace.

TO HEAL YOURSELF, EXPRESS YOUR DEEPEST DREAM.

It is time for women and men to express their dreams. There is a dream in everyone. For Mary it is to be a dancer. In her deepest dreams, she dances across the nighttime sky without limits. She moves in freedom as a transparent spiritual body, she is limber, she has no limits. "This is freeing, this image. It allows my spirit to soar and merge with Her. In my dream of being a dancer- She moves into me. By evoking Her, I invoke the deep powerful ancient feminine force. When I get large in visionary space, I feel swirling energy spiral through me, Her life force goes up in me, the feeling I have is I am being penetrated, She goes up inside me and I get larger. It is an empowering experience as we receive."

Women and men are part of a movement forward in space and time. We move with determination and deep inner knowing, with a wisdom that can be seen and felt. This wisdom may not be recognized in the normal casual interchanges in life, but the spirit of each recognizes the other, even if the personality does not connect. As we move forward with an open heart, with love and the intention for peace, we connect with each person we meet at a soul level. Woman and man merge, the life force emerges, and babies are born, not war.

Mary tells her deepest dream:

"I have this dream. Women have lunar cycles in their bodies, they have the moon. Their bodies also move with the energy of the earth. They have seasons in their bodies... as they live their lives, they respond to winds, weather, colors. These changes are reflected in their bodies. The cycles of nature that are reflected in women are their gift to men. As women and men join for peace, the earth speaks and is healed. So beautiful, this dream, so beautiful."

CHAPTER SEVEN

CARITAS PROCESS 4. TRUST AND FAITH FOR PEACE

You can shift the world's consciousness.

Trust is about developing trusting, helping, caring relationships. Let the conviction of your own truth empower you to right action. Let it come from the place of power in your belly. Let it emerge from your center in pure form. Go to the conviction of your own truth and harness that power and bring it out from your belly like a beam of light. The world needs you right now- don't doubt it for one second. Your conviction is like a psychic laser beam of light for the truth. Express it fully in right action. This is how your life manifests your choice for peace. Take your conviction for truth, place it in your gut. Place it in the place from which you know you can move forward. Express your pure truth for peace in any form you can- through teaching others, in church, in your business, in conversations with friends, in art, in political action, in civil disobedience. Empower your conviction- you are not alone- you are part of a collective of merging consciousness. You can change thought and action with this.

Let us turn the crises in the moment into the best thing that has happened. For the first time in history, people all over the earth are seriously questioning war. For the first time, people are seriously asking themselves if war is an answer, if war can be stopped, it war is a way of being that can continue on earth. Illness can be a powerful force for change. A life threatening illness such as Cancer can change a person's priorities in a moment. A person can decide to change his or her life, to love his family, to change work, to move. Ask yourself what you would do if you had one year to live, one month to live, one week to live. This question is not academic. Cancer patients ask themselves this each day. What are your priorities? This crisis is a timely doorway. Let us not turn away from it. Let it bring unity for peace and empowerment to individuals all over the earth.

Make peace with the energy of the life force.

Imagine women whirling in the nighttime sky. See them expand from their bodies and become tall. See the energy moving outward, embracing them in an aura of expanding color and wave energy. We are the women of our vision. We can use our expanding colored auric field of energy as the force to envelop others with love and compassion. One way to do this is by prayer. You pray straight forward, to the target with energy, not your energy, but universal energy. Use the life force. We have infinite resources available within our spaciousness. We are large and bright. We are illuminated in the light of our world. We are awake. Presence is our power, all we have to do is be present and see through oppression, evil, and greed and act. Trust, trust, trust yourself, for you are the embodiment of the feminine power of this dream.

We need women and men as one to make peace in the world. Men bring organization, clarity, linear placement of thoughts, this is essential for bridges of communication. Women whirl with life force and energy. As we whirl, we sprinkle stars from our own bodies. All the people are born from this energy. Women have given birth to everyone who is on earth. Think of that. Now, spiritual women twirl in sky and give birth to stars, light flows from within the stars and that is the birth of it all. Now we will give birth to peace.

RECEIVING AND GIVING

Receiving and giving in relationships is a key to this book. We move back and forth, we twirl around and around. You have been brought together on this earth to do work, to make change. Is the change you are bought here for to make world peace? Each person has a purpose and a meaning. Many people feel they are meant to accomplish something... is your job world peace? For all of us who believe in service, life is about giving and receiving. Is your work about helping mothers and children, HIV or cancer patients? Each of us has been sent to help people connect to the earth and to give to the earth. Peace is for the earth and all its children.

Walk your own path of peace in the essence of being in love. Take the same energy, the essence of being lovers, the sacred giving and receiving, the power of giving birth to life, the sacredness of giving your baby as your offering to earth, and make it a life work for peace. (Don't let any ruler take your baby for oil, political power or greed)

Lovers know the true path to peace is giving and receiving. The act of love and making the children of the world is the lover's offering. Men need to protect the world by being still and letting women teach about receiving and giving.

We cannot allow destruction of this energy. We cannot tolerate the destruction of women on earth. They are our mothers; this is the time to honor them.

This is a book about empowering you to stand up for yourself, for each other, for your children and lovers. Speak from a place of wisdom and do right action for peace.

Many people have done right action for peace. In this crisis the internet expresses the human collective noosphere for peace. Below are examples of some beautiful work for peace. We put them here to encourage you to do your own creative part for peace.

RITUALS FOR PEACE

Rituals are the most ancient method of being in contact with a higher force or power. Rituals strengthen faith but making prayer an embodied activity. Faith is believing in the fundamental goodness or positive outcomes; whatever is meant to happen happens. Even in the darkness there are opportunities for realizations and revelations. Having faith, trust in the ultimate goodness and peaceful solutions.

Ritual is a repetitive action that, combined with prayer, is believed to make change. When ritual is done with a group it becomes ceremony and the power increases. Ritual creates spiritual awareness for a purpose. Prayer and ceremony hold a magic and power that cannot be denied. Through ritual we address metaphysical energies that surround us, protect us, enliven us, and instruct us. It is the simplest way of requesting help with our problems. The ritual state of consciousness is a deeper state of being that isn't rooted in personality. A state of ecstatic union with nature is best expressed in poetry or song. In ritual and prayer, the individual who invites peace can change the world.

Peace ceremonies are a group activity. How you approach ceremony is critical. It's crucial that you approach with respect to God, the creator. How to improvise is something you learn. Holding a ceremony makes change. There are not any scripts for a ceremony. The only script is from divine intervention and guidance. Each Caritas peacemaker picks and chooses from different traditions, using a combination of what works for them. From the beginning of human experience, ceremony has been used to implement change through spiritual means. God comes to ceremonies. There are basic elements to ritual that each Caritas peacemaker or healer uses.

RITUAL ELEMENTS

- Prayer: call in God the Creator and helpers, teachers and ancestors.
- Give thanks for your life, the day, your ability to make peace.
- Ask for help with a defined intent.
- Give an offering (our offering is our lives.)
- Create sacred space with prayer and sacred objects.
- Look to the directions (some cultures).
- Go into visionary space inward to God or your wisdom within.
- Invite visions and prayers to come.
- Drumming and music, songs and prayer are common.
- In peace, let the voices of wisdom come to you.
- Let go and release illness, suffering, and war.
- Invite cleansing and purification.

- In closing, give thanks again and strengthen community with contact with others.

THE STEPS FOR MANIFESTING CHANGE WITH CEREMONY

- Go inward to glimpse the wisdom vision.
- Listen to wisdom voices.
- Coming out with resolve and trust.
- Clarify your intent.
- Focus your plan.
- Get together your tools.
- Manifest right action.

DEALING WITH EXHAUSTION AND DARKNESS ??

In powerful peace work there is great energy being moved. Sometimes, afterwards it is raw. It is as if the hard work pushes the Caritas peacemaker over the edge. What makes the life of the Caritas peacemaker balance? How can the Caritas peacemaker live a life where she or he is working for peace all the time? How can he or she keep functioning at a high level and maintain their own health? What allows them to do this work and not burn out or get ill? The answer is getting energy from the outside and releasing pain. Energy from the earth keeps you well, and rest and transitions afterwards ground you and bring you back. Releasing suffering to the earth purifies and cleanses you to start afresh.

- Offer prayer.
- Get ready and work hard.
- Understand you are in an altered state which requires huge energy.
- Rest up and afterward sleep.
- Protect yourself with prayer and imagery.

- Come out of hard work slowly.
- Deal with fear.
- Release and let go of suffering, do not carry it home, let the earth take it.
- Deal with your own issues and blocks before or afterward, deprocess.
- Remember forgiveness and acceptance of ourselves and others.

A GUIDED IMAGERY FOR A PEACE CIRCLE RITUAL

We have performed this ritual in groups during the last year for peace. We did it in large community stone circle before the war. It was very beautiful. We include it as an example of a ritual so you can make your own ceremony with your group. We frame the ritual as a guided imagery so you can picture it in your mind's eye.

You stand in the center of a circle of women and men. The women form a circle in the center and men a second circle around them- supporting them to foster a nurturing view for world peace. The women are the ancient mothers to the earth, the men ancient fathers. The feminine and masculine energies merge together to make world peace.

For women: Imagine yourself in an inner circle with men in an outer circle around you. In the inner circle you are surrounded by the ancient mothers of earth. They are from all over the world, all over the earth... there are old women from Africa, Celtic women, old women from Sicily. In your mind's eye see the old women from different places in the world, from China, South America; see a community of women from the world's spiritualities... see Christian, Buddhist, Hindu, Jewish, Islam woman... all these women from the world are the ancient mothers of the earth.

These women call to you, they call to you to give birth to world peace now. They are your own ancient grandmothers. They tell you, take control, be women of power, make peace, do not tolerate the patriarchy. Look at the mess they made. We look to you as our grand daughters, you are our way of being. It has taken this long for this to happen. It has taken this long for you to get the power to take over the world. Many of the ancient women came from little villages, they did not leave the village their whole lives. You travel the earth weaving webs of peace. We are part of this lineage of ancient mothers. As we become an ancient mother, our mission is to protect our children. This means all the children of the earth. All children are our children, all children are our concern, the earth is our family.

For men: Imagine yourself in an outer circle around the women inner circle. In this outer circle you are surrounded by the ancient fathers of earth. They are from all over the world, all over the earth… there are old men from Africa, Celtic men, old men from Sicily. In your mind's eye see the old men from different places in the world, from China, South America; see a community of men from the world's spiritualities… see Christian, Buddhist, Hindu, Jewish, Islam men… all these men from the world are the ancient fathers of the earth.

These men call to you, they call to you to give birth to world peace now. They are your own ancient grandfathers. They tell you this is a new time, do not make the patriarchal mistakes we made. Look at the earth at war now. We did this. We apologize for this. We look to you as our grandsons, you are our way of being. It has taken this long for this to happen. It has taken this long for you to get the power to take over the world and create endless wars. It is time you stopped. Pause for a moment, look into the center circle. See how beautiful the women are. Honor the feminine now, let them create peace, support them and stand back. Many of the ancient men came from little villages, they did not leave the village their whole lives. You travel the earth weaving webs of peace. We are part of the lineage of ancient fathers. As we become an ancient father, our mission is to protect our children. This means all the children of the earth. All children are our children, all children are our concern; the earth is our family.

Now, imagine the circles start to rotate clockwise. The women's circle starts to slowly turn and the man's circle goes around them. Now as the circles spin, look at each other with love. Thank the women for creating peace, thank the men for supporting them, honoring them and listening to their voices. Now make one big circle; let the feminine and masculine energy merge. Look with love at each other. Together you are the life force, the way new life is created, not destroyed.

EXPERIENCING TRANSCENDENCE FOR PEACE

Transcendence is the experience of something greater. Transcendence is the lived experience of something so powerful that trust and faith are deeply strengthened…to heal from visions of darkness, experience feelings of oneness, feelings of an immense interconnectedness. Connectedness and oneness purify the spirit from dark images. Glimpse God or angels; experience the power of the universe or God. Feel yourself in the presence of God, and hear the voice of God. Emerge in another dimension, one of great power and beauty. Transcendence is hearing a message from God. You are a vehicle to share love, to communicate love. Experience transformation… see yourself for the first time, discover within yourself a place of ecstasy. Let yourself become filled with power or light

A major help for a Caritas peacemaker is to experience transcendence. The experience of a peak spiritual event is possible for anyone who wants this to happen. It is not the province of the spiritual adept, it is for anyone who meditates and prays.

If the messages from God that you receive in meditation or prayer are to go to war or kill others- you are not going deep enough. You are involved in your ego and not hearing the voice of God. All spiritual leaders will tell you God is peace and love, not a voice of war. Man turns God's word to war for his own greed and gain. Woman turns it back to peace.

Exercises for experiencing transcendence

Your life as a Caritas peacemaker is an embodied prayer. Your work is your embodied prayer. From the first glimpse of God or your spirit from within your pain, your entire journey is an embodied prayer. Each act is part of your prayer for peace, part of your prayer of thanks, part of your prayer to heal others and the earth.

Transcendence is a visionary experience; let a shape that is in natural forms trigger a memory of spirit from deep inside you. This is how the artist works, he gets ideas from abstract shapes around them. The sculptor sees a piece of wood and gets the idea of the sculpture she carves from the grain pattern. He sees it in the wood. The image seen in the shape is the germ of the spiritual vision. When a vision appears, let yourself see it. Let yourself see beauty, let yourself see spirit. Seeing a vision is a letting go, an acceptance, an honoring, an invitation. Go into places in your inner world of meditation and prayer that are beyond time and space. Feel the place of no space and no time. Timelessness is a feeling.

The sacred space of prayer and vision has characteristics. There are certain visions that are seen by many spiritual people or mediators. Cracking, sizzling, opening areas, light, flames, borders all are common. When you look for spirit, look for these things. When you look at paintings of religious themes, you see halos, flames, light rays. Look at the work of visionary artists like Alex Grey. His portrayal of space is close to what patients who are near death tell us they see. Lines of electricity, lightning, areas of white light, jewels. Look at pictures of God or religious figures painted by visionary artists. Collect the pictures and hang them around you. Put them where you can see them when you wake and go to sleep. Hang them in your office or peace headquarters. Listen to sacred music. Invite peak spiritual visions to come to inform you about peace and your role as a Caritas peacemaker.

When you are in conflict or war, merging with another is a powerful healing tool. When the love and light that is within you merges with the love and light from another person, it magnifies and deepens and becomes extraordinarily powerful. Ego is blown away, contact of souls is beyond thought, deep into the heart. If you are in conflict, let yourself expand and flow outwards to the enemy or people who are with you. You can make a prayer circle to magnify the energy even more. You can do this, it has been done for centuries by holy men and teachers.

ACTIVITIES FOR TRANSCENDENCE

To experience the awakening to the sacred, awaken to nature. Go into the silence of a foggy dawn, go into the actual energy of silence, go into the opening light of the new day. Spirit appears in such places. Involve your senses of smell, touch, feel yourself moving through space and time. It involves a shift in your ability to see. It is about being mindfully present to spirit.

To create sacred space to make peace in your life, say a prayer. Give thanks to the deity you believe in. Ask them to come to you and help you make peace. You can make an altar, a medicine wheel, a place where you put a sacred painting, to give you a tangible place to start. You can make a sacred place around you anywhere at any time. You carry it with you in your heart.

To experience transcendence, open your inner eyes. See the light that comes from within, with your eyes closed. As you feel yourself slip across the veil, as you feel time and space changing, be aware of the appearance of the moment of peace out of time. Look for it with beauty. As you feel it coming, it seems like space opens, expands, changes quality. It is subtle- if you have not experienced it before, each time you learn to recognize it more easily. For most people, a gray light appears, a voice or vision appears and speaks to you. You may have an intuitive understanding and knowledge that it is God, that you are in the presence of God. Don't be afraid or put yourself down and say you don't deserve it. Everyone deserves God's love. You have every right to see and experience the voice of God, angels, Blessed Mother. Crucial to having the experience is letting it come to you without extinguishing it with fear or judgment. If you believe it can happen to you, it will; if you think it can only happen to saints, you will not allow yourself to accept the vision when it starts to come.

Look especially for the experience of illuminosity, the experience of the light within and without as one. It is described as a radiance from within itself, not from the sun. It can be as much of a feeling as a vision, you can notice it afterwards as you think about it, or during the vision. When you see or hear the voice or vision, expect a message. You will often receive a message from God to you about how to heal and who you are and what to do, not just experience a vision. It often helps to create an event where spirit will enter, where transcendence will appear. Dance, music, art, prayer, nature all make it more likely. A ritual and a ritual repeated with other people make it more likely to happen.

THE DOVE

The dove is a universal symbol of peace. It has been seen in visions of peace for thousands of years. It appears in mediation and in visions. It is often seen with a blue border surrounded by flames. In ancient Greek mythology the dove was the bird of Athena which represented the renewal of life. In the Bible, the dove was released from the Ark by Noah. The dove returned with an olive branch to show that the Biblical flood was over. The dove symbolizes deliverance and God's forgiveness.

"At the end of forty days, after the flood, Noah opened the window of the ark that he had made and sent out the raven to see if it could find dry land; and it went to and fro until the waters were dried up from the earth. Then he sent out the dove from him, to see if the waters had subsided from the face of the ground; but the dove found no place to set its foot, and it returned to him to the ark, for the waters were still on the face of the whole earth. So he put out his hand and took it and brought it into the ark with him. He waited another seven days and again he sent out the dove from the ark; and the dove came back to him in the evening, and there in its beak was a freshly plucked olive leaf; so Noah knew that the waters had subsided from the earth. Then he waited another seven days, and sent out the dove; and it did not return to him any more." *(Genesis 8:6-12).*

The dove, taken by Christianity as the emblem of the Holy Ghost, was originally an extremely ancient pagan female emblem that was seen in visions and revered. In many ancient traditions it represented the mother who made the world. The dove was the deity who symbolized the procreative functions of love and childbirth. Because of its gentleness and devotion to its babies, the dove was seen as the embodiment of the mother and of feminine nurturing energy. In mythology the dove is worshipped by the Great Mother Goddesses and as femininity and maternity. The dove was sacred to Astarte, Cybele, Isis,Venus, Juno, Mylitta, and Aphrodite. The dove is also an emblem of wisdom, since it stands for the power of manifestation. It also has been thought of as a messenger of the divine.

A vision of a dove is a vision of peace. Ask a dove to come to you and be with you as you walk *The Path to a Peaceful Life.*

GATHER THE CARITAS PEACEMAKERS TOGETHER FOR PEACE

We believe the new world will manifest from people's dreams of beauty and peace. Only peace allows us to envelop the tapestry of a full rich life. Peace creates space for life to grow and flourish. Peace creates the place where the human collective evolves to God. War creates death, in war there is no space for life. It is simple… war destroys our place, steals our life, make us victims and prisoners in this life. We don't want that to happen to anyone anymore, we don't want this to happen to any of our women and children.

What we do to others will come back to us. What goes around comes around, what we put out comes back ten fold. That is a natural law. When we perpetuate destruction, we destroy. When we take things apart with destruction, we are destroyed within, damaged for life. When we birth forms with the God given life giving force, we create.

Those are the two paths, it is our choice to follow the path of the life giving force. That force is within us. It is another law of the universe. The life force births forms, those who give birth do not fight wars. Their force is to use their mind to create world peace.

Gather in community to create beauty, home, to nurture. Gather as women and nurturing peace-loving men to make food, to make a hearth. This is what we need to empower ourselves to do. Gather together to create a safe place for our women and children. Gather on the earth to intensify the life giving force and gather for our children. Our children are our daughters and sons, our children are our businesses, our children are our peace projects. We are the mothers and fathers of all we create; we do know the wisdom of earth with in us. It makes perfect sense, you do not have to learn anything. You only need to remember you are women and men here to heal the earth. Our gift and our offering is ourselves and our wisdom. We walk *The Path to a Peaceful Life*. We are all teachers, all speakers, all mothers, all fathers all doers, all knowers, all Caritas peacemakers for Peace.

We invite you to become a crucial part of the global consciousness for world peace. Let us together articulate the world vision, the brilliance of world peace. Let us make the choice to be part of this real unified movement for change. Let us create a new consensual reality where peace is the only way to solve problems; and social justice, respect for diversity and equality is real, not just rhetoric. If enough of us make the choice for peace, it will happen and we will change the world by what we think. The commitment of our life is what we offer- our life is our offering- our offering is our life. The path to peace needs you- it needs everyone from poets to parents. The whole community needs to be involved. We need your life, your creativity and your passion. Passion is the life force that will make it happen. The force of destruction is powerful; we need our life force to move into the unknown and manifest peace in space and form in our lives. Let us make our lives our embodied prayers for peace- it takes practice every day. "Blessed are the Caritas peacemakers for Peace, for they will be called sons of God" (Matthew 5:9).

CHAPTER EIGHT

CARITAS PROCESS 5. FORGIVENESS: ALLOWING THE EXPRESSING OF POSITIVE AND NEGATIVE FEELINGS

Forgiveness is a crucial step in creating peace. Forgiveness is about promoting and accepting the positive and negative feelings as you authentically listen to another story. Self forgiveness is the first step in creating inner piece. First, forgive yourself for not being the person you want to be. Forgive yourself for your apathy, your lack of concern, your turning away from people in need. Forgive yourself for doing business and not making enough time for family and loved ones. Forgive yourself for not feeding the hungry and working for peace. Forgive yourself for not stopping the war. Move on to become a Caritas peacemaker now. Accept and love yourself for your own imperfections.

FORGIVING OURSELVES

In self forgiveness you find the ability to create sacred space and clarity. In self forgiveness you give yourself room to create a life of freedom. Forgiveness is an active process. Revenge is the opposite of forgiveness, it breeds endless war. Revenge now is alive; thousands of years after events in the middle East and Europe have ended, it creates new wars daily. This is not the first war of the twenty first century. There are many on earth already from ancient revenge.

Love does not instantly change everything, but acting out of love does heal your own life.

Compassion leads to self healing. Seeing yourself with compassion heals the pain and darkness in your own life.

To forgive yourself, it is necessary to look at what you have done and not done. The enemy tells us this. If you look out of the eyes of your adversary you see yourself in a different way. In this crisis we must look at why we are hated. The messages are clear, not hidden. They do not justify terrorism but they tell us why it happened and give us messages on how it can be prevented. To forgive ourselves we need to listen to our enemy and see what we can change. Social change prevents war.

MARY'S STORY OF FORGIVENESS

Mary tells this personal story of forgiveness. It is not about war or killing but it is about forgiveness:

"It was hard for me when my husband left me. It was a betrayal, but something had to happen. In the situation he was in, he had fallen into his own darkness; he felt betrayed, used, unappreciated. He felt he was enslaved and had no choices left. He felt he was failing. He had always wanted to be a good husband and father and doctor, he could not face the pain of his own inadequacy. Then a younger and seductive woman appeared, and I could see what was going to happen. It was as if the trap was set. He was going to leave me and my little daughter and son. They needed him so badly, they would cry and daddy would not come home. He worked all the time and he was too tired. As time went on my husband was getting sicker and sicker. I said he was sick, and he said he was not. He denied everything. I begged him to do something different. When he had fallen in love it was now a new beginning for him. There was a part of me that felt it had to happen, we could not go on. He did not see me, he did not feel my love anymore. We were in a cold violent storm, we were being beaten by life and each other and we both were failing. The greatest sadness of the moment was the children had lost us both.

There were times I would hold them and not let them go. He would have to peel them off my body. I screamed, "You cannot take them, you cannot take my children." He would put them in the car anyway. "I will not let you take the children, you can run me right over," and I would stand in front of the car. I could see the children's confusion, they wanted to be with their dad. They loved us both. After they left, I would stand in the driveway for hours and hours and I would scream. I felt so violated. I was so unhappy and so hurt, I could see in their faces that they saw everything. They saw all the misery and all the violence. I would just scream. It was awful, I had lost my mind. When my children were gone, I would become suicidal. Then, in the house of my darkness, I would face my mothers' menacing voice. She would point her finger and harp at me, "You shouldn't do that in front of the children. What effect will this have for the children? You are hurting your own children. You should be ashamed of yourself. Shame, shame, shame on you. " All I could think of was not being there, being dead, they won't see me, but in another part of me I can't believe this I really happening.

I could barely make it through the days, I remember they were sunny. I did crazy things of unbridled rage and terror. I would go there without fear, I was destroying myself. To try to heal I would go on retreats and go into silence and just be with my sadness, just sit with my pain. During that time, I relived all of the most painful memories, memories of my childhood, of my back breaking, of being strangled, and raped; they were real memories, I was not making them up. I was shocked as I remembered it all. I had experiences so painful, and I was a mess, I was one hurt on top of another. It was amazing I could still live.

The reason I am telling you this story is simple, it is about forgiveness. After two years of excruciating pain and after finally letting go from pure exhaustion, I remember the night my husband knocked on the door. He stood there and asked me if he could come back. I opened the door and I was totally empty. I could see his despair and fear, I could see he was still traveling in corridors of madness. I was in stillness; it was over, my madness. I looked at him. "Will you forgive me?" he said,. and I said, "Of course I will forgive you". I thought to myself, it is nothing compared to what I need to be forgiven for. I will forgive him and I will forget,: I will let allow life to be what it is . I realized I had learned about surrender and compassion. I learned how to forgive and how to let go. I learned how to have faith in a new day, in what will come to me that I could not see. I offered my life to be whatever it would be and was meant to be, not necessarily what I thought I wanted.

Forgiveness is a gift to be given for you. Forgiveness is letting go. Forgiveness is a gift you give yourself that heals the rage, hurt, pain, and resentment. It makes room for a brand new day. Let go of your hurt, embrace the light in your life like the morning sun."

GIFT OF LISTENING

Listening is a practice of giving and receiving. Listening is an act that takes energy and attention. Listening is looking into the eyes of the other or at least a gentle gaze on the other person's presence. It is an active engagement that requires attention. Listening can be a peaceful, beautiful experience. Allow yourself to listen to the sound, tone, words, feeling the feeling being communicated gently opening the heart and acknowledging the others words feelings and thought. Allow your own body to be peace and spaciousness. Cultivate a stillness within, allowing your own thoughts to recede, and empty yourself of your own feelings, creating a pause. In this pause allow moment to lengthen, cultivate a feeling that within this moment all eternity exists and all that this is. Your presence is a gift to the other where you become available with your body with your time and in their space. Activating how you listen requires your body to be and your heart to be open. It is an opportunity to connect heart to heart, spirit to spirit.. . it requires allowing everything to be just is it is with nothing added, purely the purity of being of peace and receiving. Pure authentic listening requires removing any negative filters, disinterest, boredom, conclusions, judgment, arrogance, frustration, defensiveness. More than seeking meaning, and clarification or validation of someone, it is listening for the authentic expression of being, something more. It's allowing something to be what it is, having faith and trust and believing things are exactly as they are meant to be.

EMPLOY THE ETHICS OF FACE TO FORGIVE YOUR ENEMY

- The face is the most compelling part of someone.
- The face invites you to respond.
- Be responsive to gestures.
- Look into the eyes, look at the skin, look at the light around their head, notice their hair.

- A piercing gaze has appeal.
- To turn away is insult.

ACTIVE LISTENING AND FORGIVENESS

Active listening is an important skill for the Caritas peacemaker. With it you can very sensitively listen to how people feel- this includes your enemy. Active listening helps bring forgiveness. It allows you to understand the other person's point of view and see their humanity below their anger or hate.

To practice active listening you say, "Tell me how things are for you." Then you respond to the feeling words such as hurt, abused, ignored, insulted, attacked, . then repeat the last feeling word, e.g. "attacked" and paraphrase what you understand happened. "It sounds to me like when this happened, you expected something different." The paraphrase has feeling, content, and meaning to the person. For example, "You just said some important things, let's see if I understand what you said. Is this what you were sayin?." Reflect it, repeat it. The process only needs five minutes. The person can release a great deal in this time. You can say, "You went though a lot." Process it, open up communication about their feelings.

Tools for active listening to an adversary

- Paraphrase what they said.
- Reflect it back to them with respect.
- Validate their feelings with honor.
- Work together for a creative solution.
- To lesson anger remember a time when you both were happy, comfortable and safe.
- Use imagery with a beginning, middle, and end of the war to see past the darkness.
- Help them imagine a time when they met a challenge and use that energy for peace.

- Breathe, gaze gently, and hold space.

When stuck in darkness, fear or anger:

- What is happening right now that makes it hard?
- Understand together that this is a scary time.
- Get into a safe place where you both as adults can be here now.
- Understand, this is hard for both of us, let's have courage.
- Can we each remember a time when we met a challenge and take that energy for peace?
- Move always at the other's pace.
- Find out where the other is and help them to move to where they want to go.
- Remember, each person has a different life experience.
- You need to be comfortable with silence.
- You need to be comfortable with tears- let it happen.
- Realize in an embodied way what the other person feels, feel it in your body.

You are dealing with a complex wonderful human being with his point of view. All you can do is be there with them. Say, "Tell me what you are experiencing right now." You need to know their feelings to see out of their eyes and to make peace.

HELPING AFTER A TRAUMATIC SITUATION:

- Listen to the person's story, process it, experience it.
- Let the person know they are heard, honored and respected.
- Restory their participation in your own word back to them.
- First debriefing, how did the incident happen?
- Help calm them down with love and respect.

- Normalizing their feelings will help.
- Ask them, "Are things we can do to solve the conflict?"

INTERVENTIONS FOR CHANGE:

- Imagine a place of peace.
- Imagine a safe place.
- Contain negative feelings in a bubble when necessary.
- Get a massage.
- Write the story of your pain.
- Write letters never sent to your adversary.
- Talk to an empty chair to let it out.
- Use creativity to find new interventions.

DEALING WITH DEATH AND EVIL

Violence is about going into the underworld. The underworld is each of our own inner of outer worlds of darkness, pain, and suffering. The underworld is our place of our fear of death. It is the world that comes from our personality, our conditioning and our family's habits. It comes from our father and mother and grandfather and grandmother's sadness, disappointment, suffering, rage and fear. It comes from racial memories or war, of experiences of war told to us by relatives and friends, of books and movies on war. It is the fear of the knocking on the door, the soldiers overrunning a village, the bombs falling, the men being shot and women being raped. It has happened since the beginning of cities and agriculture. It is the old way of being.

Those that are living walk in the depths of death and loss daily. There are deaths daily. A monumental death is no differ than daily death. As a person and as a community we need to know how to deal with death. We need to take out our feelings of rage and non- acceptance and let them transform.

Do we walk forward? How do we deal with death responsibly? How do we create pain? We are simply God's children, we are spiritual people. We live the challenge of life. Inside darkness is the potential for spiritual evolution.

LOOK AT DARKNESS AND DEATH WITH YOUR INNER VOICE OF WISDOM

Go into your darkness and fears with your inner voice of wisdom. The underworld is in the deepest crevices and darkest shadows of the earth and your own soul. This deep place within can be so dark that no meditator or devotee would go in without their teacher or inner guide. There are many things happening to you when you go into your own underworld. Suffering, pain, death and the darkness exist in the world.

As you are willing to go into the darkness within the corridors in your own mind, you can face thinking about real war. The wounded events in your past, the patterns that are dysfunctional in your life, the legacies of recurring themes from your grandmother are the spirits of your darkness. Lay down your life and be willing to go into the darkness.

The darkness is in the very cells of your body. The prisons are in your own mind. Be with them and merge with them. There are wrinkles of darkness all though your life, all through your body. Be willing to flow on the pathway into your soul… see who you are under the mask you present to the world. Take all your control issues and fears and vanquish them. That is what going to the underground is about. Walk into your fears, and if you can do that you will not be afraid of anything inside yourself or inside of another. Then you can walk into the prisms of light you are capable of manifesting in this lifetime, and be a healer to others.

As you deal with your own negativity and lack of faith, you will become a channel of grace. Let go and have faith in the process. Darkness manifests in the world as bad events and people. War is the ultimate darkness. The underworld is about indulging the self verses selflessness. Go into the primal darkness of your own fears. Flow down the river unfettered. Take in the fresh experience of whatever is happening without fear.

To go through the darkness, allow the fears and visions to burn out. Allow it to happen and let it burn out your karmic trappings. Allow debts to be repaid, honor the suffering you are given. The earth is trying to wake you up. To understand the suffering of the earth, is what feeling our own suffering is for. We are evolving as more sensitive beings, and now the planet is suffering. Nothing has ever needed us like this. The earth needs us like we are now. All our visions are from the earth to wake us up.

The oracles always had a dark side. They always had a card that was turned over, that said, do not cross the great water, do not do this. This is about man's control. The flood is about man not being able to control the waters. It is good that man cannot control everything. Otherwise he would destroy the earth.

ABOUT PROTECTION

For every person dealing with darkness, there is an issue of protection. Intentionally creating a Caritas field creates an energetic space that protects you. Prayer and teachers create a spiral that acts as a veil that protects you. When you go into visionary space where you are open, you are vulnerable. You need protection and guardians. The guides and teachers hold the space, keep you grounded, maintain space and time. They take care of you, love you, and protect you.

ALL HUMANS CARRY PAIN

All humans carry pain. We all carry a legacy of abuse. The animals never killed each other for sport, they never had wars, they never massacred each other by the thousands or millions. Our ancestors did this. When you see visions of the past you do not see your ancestors in the place they were in when they were at war unless you are at war. You see them in a place inside yourself that has no judgment, no guilt. It is not about apologizing; you see them in the clearest space possible. What they transcend, you transcend as you see them. When you look into ancient eyes they are not angry. The time has come to listen to the earth. Human nature needs to be healed, the violence needs to be healed. What is done in the present moment can literally liberate the past.

EVIL AND DARKNESS

Teachers tell us their own views of evil. Spiritual teachers have different beliefs that span from not believing that evil is real to believing it is one side of God. In war, our leaders always tell us the enemy is evil and we are good. It is important to face evil and learn what it actually is. Meditators face darkness and evil. For Chardin, for example the conquest of evil is only secondary to the purpose of evolution . Evil is described by Teilhard de Chardin as growing pains in the cosmic process: the disorder that is implied by order in process of realization. This non judgmental view could not take a person to war but would help problem solve for peace.

CHARDIN'S VIEW OF EVIL

Chardin has a non judgmental view of evil that prevents evil being used as an excuse for war. He believes that humans, as a part of the cosmic oneness travel the evolutionary path, "grasping and growing, making mistakes but yet achieving mastery. Humanity is body and mind, manifest and nonmanifest. Humanity is not whole, but knows that it can be Whole. Humanity is a great mystery. In humanity's immediate world there is evil and evolution. There is ignorance along with consciousness and creativity. And war and destruction accompany the construction of civilization."

Chardin talked about evil in the cosmic process. He described the different categories of evil: "The Evil of Disorder and Failure is engendered by a cosmic process that is groping, taking chances, and making choices. The Evil of Decomposition, which is sickness and corruption, results from some "unhappy chance," and death, which exists because of the "indispensable condition of the re-placement of one individual by another along a phyletic stem." The Evil of Solitude and Anxiety is basically the great anxiety of a "consciousness wakening up to reflection." And the Evil of Growth is that which is symbolically suffered in the "pangs of childbirth."

Chardin especially considered that the concept of *original sin* "translates, personifies...the perennial and universal law of imperfec-tion which operates in mankind in virtue of its being in the process of becoming." Salvation beckons for Chardin, precisely because evil (disorder) is perceived to be caused, because the "creature... along with the cosmos...is in process". He believes that once this perception is fully understood, we will be able to understand the other side of this evil. Chardin said that "Evil, in all its forms...injustice, inequality, suffering, death...ceases theoretically to be outrageous from the mo-ment when *Evolution becoming a Genesis*... displays itself as the...price of an *immense triumph*." Then life on this planet will no longer seem a "meaningless prison," but rather the "matrix in which our unity is be-ing forged."

For Chardin, the tragic, real evil in this life occurs when humanity fails to acquire a sense of the true value of the universe. Teilhard portends that for the "man who sees nothing at the end of the world, nothing higher than himself, (than) daily life can only be filled with pettiness and boredom."

The way beyond the ignorance, for Chardin, is basically an individuation process. He regrets that the human ego must make the pilgrimage into *Self*. He says it thus: "my ego must subsist through abandoning itself or the gift will fade away." The gift is the Self. It is the "very center of our consciousness...that is the essence which Omega, if it is to be truly Omega, must reclaim." Chardin is not asking the human ego to self-destruct; rather, by climbing to a higher level of consciousness the ego becomes greater. The more the ego is connected with a sense of cosmic insight, the more it finds its true Self...and via the Self the more connected humanity becomes with the Cosmic Mind.

To be fully ourselves, according to Teilhard, we must head in the direction of "convergence with all the rest...towards the other." He puts it grandly: "The peak of ourselves, the acme of our originality, is not our individuality but our person; and according to the evolution-ary structure of the world, we can only find our person by uniting together. There is no mind without synthesis."

The most important point of Teilhard's vision is that the "*point of the cosmos is to achieve multidimensional wholeness.* Humanity, as an aspect of the cosmos, is part and parcel to this process towards whole-ness." Thus going apart from oneness, is the problem, separating from another human and calling him evil is the problem, not evil as a inde-pendent entity itself. We cannot go to war for good and against evil if evil is separateness and moving against evolution.

GUIDED IMAGERY TO HONOR SUFFERING

Again, start by finding a comfortable place to go through the process you have found that takes you into meditation and deep relaxation. Let these feelings of relaxation spread throughout your body and let your relaxation deepen with each breath.

In your mind's eye picture yourself working for peace. Let the love you feel come to you and surround you. Be in the love and compas-sion you have from the universe. Now imagine you are the most compassionate person you have known, heard of, read about or imagined. It can be Jesus, Mother Mary, the Dalai Lama, Buddha, God. Go up into them, merge with them and be in their heart. Let the love you are merge with the love they are and be one. Now look at the person you are with in pure compassion. Look at them through the eyes of the compassionate one. Look at them through the eyes of your deepest love and compassion.

Now imagine the person you are with tells you a story of great suffering or pain. It can be of war, or of something that was done to them or their country. You can remember a story that you have heard in your peace work or let a new one appear in your imagination. As you hear this story, let your love and compassion surround you and the person you are with like a blanket from a mother to her baby. Let the love flow into the person from the compassionate one inside you, from you into them. While you do this, do not interrupt the person's story, do not stop them from crying, just be there with them in perfect peace.

When you are ready, return to the room and do your de-compression process. You are back, you can carry the experience of the exercise outward to your life. You will feel stronger and be able to see deeper. You will be in a healing state. Each time you do the exercise you will be more relaxed and be able to go deeper in your work for peace.

CHAPTER NINE

CARITAS PROCESS 6. CREATIVITY AND PEACE

ART IS THE MANIFESTATION OF OUR VISIONS FOR PEACE

Creativity is about creating solutions and caring decision-making for peace. Use your creative life force to become a source of inspiration and energy that propels you to co create Caritas fields of peace with others. The creative process will give you the energy to increase the energy of this vibration with passion. Passion helps you tap into the eternal spring of creativity that flows within you as naturally as the spring flow from the earth.. We are the earth…our creativity connects with the earth. Tap into the vortex of your creative energy. When you tap into the power of creativity, it flows through you, nurtures you and heals you. As your creativity emerges through you, it heals the earth as it emerges from the earth. Making art is healing in itself. Making art for peace is the earth making peace.

Prayer, art and healing come from the same place: the human soul. The creation of art is an act of prayer in which we create harmony and balance within ourselves through the extrinsic movement between the inner and outer world. In the creation of art, we respond to our hopes and problems in a creative way. We create images that emerge from our soul in response to our dreams and visions. We take a vision from our wisdom within and externalize it so everyone can see it. We manifest creative reality from the inner world. Art was transformative in ancient times; it was the way the shaman helped control the hunt, fertility and even the weather. Art changes reality by transforming consciousness.

The Caritas peacemaker makes art to learn how to find creative solutions for peace, and to heal themselves so that they can make peace. The process of making art is the process of seeing into visionary space, it is the same process the Caritas peacemaker uses as he tries to get new ideas to solve problems. When a person makes art, the images that come to her or him are creative ideas. They can inform us about what to do next, about decision or actions. The art can be engaging for an audience, be a song to rally support and free emotions. A dance for peace can express emotion and move people to action.

THE TREE VISION OF THE CONTEMPORARY CARITAS PEACEMAKER

The Iroquois peacemaker had a vision of a pine tree that united the five tribes. Here is our vision of a tree to unite the contemporary Caritas peacemakers for Peace in creativity.

Imagine yourself as a giant tree. The tree has a taproot which goes deep and is connected to a spring in the earth itself. Water from the spring flows up into the tree and makes you grow. As you grow, energy from the earth spirals up through the trunk and reaches to the sun and light. The tree goes though the seasons, through fall, winter, spring and summer and is connected to the cycles of life. As the tree grows, it expands and reaches out further to the sun. As it grows, it bears fruit and gives seeds to make new life. You give your gifts of art and beauty like it gives its gifts of seeds. Your gifts of creativity are food for the soul and come from deep within you. They shower the earth as the spiral of pure water goes up through the tree towards the light. The tree has a heart which opens with love. Likewise, your gifts are given with love through your open heart. The tree can see itself, its open heart is an inner witness to its awakened consciousness. The tree is aware of itself and of the world. You are aware of yourself and of the world.

In this tree is an eagle. The eagle flies up in high graceful spirals and comes back home and lands on its branches; the tall tree is the home of eagle. The eagle can see across landscapes, the eagle is at home in and above the earth's landscapes. The eagle spirals up into the sky with freedom. The eagle's powers are yours too, the acuity of vision, the energy, the brilliance of majestic flight are also yours.

Imagine as you give, you are grounded in the earth. You too have a taproot;, your creative powers are given as fruits you give to the world. You feed the world with your art. You bless the world with beauty. You give of your very substance as the gift of who you actually are. Your creativity creates the abundance of life.

Peace is your creative gift. Through *Caritas peace book*, you give of yourself. You give your creative gifts through intention with an open heart to the world. And through your inner witness. you also give your creative gifts to yourself. Creativity helps you meet the unmet needs of the world.

A creative process is essential to empower you as a Caritas peacemaker. Your dance for peace, your art for peace, your lifework for peace are interrelated with the life force emerging. Creativity for peace transcends traditional art- in this process your most important art is your life. Your complete and mature creative process is who you are-- your life. Through the process of inner and outer transformation you reach for transcendence of pain and suffering. Your life is a work of art for peace.

A theme of artists who work for peace is making community. Honoring people and seeing them in beauty for who they are is key. Involving people in their own art and making art is a central concept. The stone sculptor Vijali Hamilton traveled around the earth making art for peace. Her World Mandala for Peace involved people in indigenous communities all over the world. She went from being a studio artist to an artist for transformation. She had a vision where she saw herself as a pilgrim for peace. One of Vijali's projects involved making art with Israeli and Palestinian children for peace. As the children got to know each other, they saw the other's point of view of beauty. Art helped them see out of the eyes of the other. You can be a pilgrim for peace in your own community. You can do creative innovative projects that have never been done before in your own neighborhood. Neighborhood artists have done projects to heal minorities, AIDS patients, elderly, women and children. They are now doing art for peace all over the earth. Art is creative, inspiration, transformative and surprising. Become an artist for peace.

VIJALI AND THE EARTH MANDALA FOR GLOBAL PEACE

Among the many artists who do their art intentionally for peace, Vijali is one of the most remarkable. Her vision, commitment and novel solutions are inspiring to everyone who sees her work. She is truly a model for creativity for peace, and her beautiful stone carvings for peace are a personal process that transforms people's consciousness. Vijali, a visionary multimedia artist, sculptor, poet, and musician is the originator of Earth Mandala. This work, a global peace project, combines sculptures in living rock and community ritual-based theater. Her work includes education, art, spirituality, peace activism, and focuses attention on the resolution of environmental, spiritual, and social problems. Earth Mandala is an artistic forum for global understanding. It activates awareness of our interconnection with all life.

Earth Mandala: (World Wheel), is an artistic forum for global understanding consisting of twelve monumental stone sculptures and ceremony performance events circling the globe on the 35th latitudinal parallel. It focuses on spiritual ecological issues, activating an awareness of the interrelatedness of all life. Through active participation with local artists, performers and community, Earth Mandala addresses the people's deepest personal and social concerns, working creatively with them to resolve cultural conflicts. Earth Mandala provides a transformative experience for the community.

The first Earth Mandala took place seven years beginning in Malibu, California and continued on to the Seneca Reservation, New York--Alicante on the Mediterranean Sea of Spain--the Umbrian Forest of Italy--the island of Tinos in Greece--the desert of Egypt--the banks of the Dead Sea in Israel and Palestine--a tiny village in West Bengal, India--a cave in Shoto Terdrom, Tibet--a national park in Kunming, Western China--on the banks of Lake Baikal, Siberia. In October of 1993 the culmination of this journey was in Japan at the ancient Shinto shrine of Tenkawa.

The motivation for the Earth Mandala came from an experience in the mid 70's when Vijali's perception of herself and the world shifted, and the Unity of life stood revealed to her. Her next few years were a search for a way to live within this web of life that connects all life. Specific ideas for the Earth Mandala came to her in a dream; "I saw myself carving sculptures out of the living rock and involving people from many culture in a process of ritual in a giant circle around the world. The circle itself represents Unity in the sense that each spoke of the wheel has a quality that is unique, distinct from every other spoke of the wheel and yet it is from these differences that harmony arises, from these differences that the whole is created.

As soon as I arrive in a country, I ask each person I meet, three questions:

1. What is our essence?
2. What is our sickness, our imbalance ... personally, communally and globally?
3. What can heal this sickness, what can bring us into balance?

Their response to these questions forms the art and ritual performance. Each earth sculpture serves as the performance space and is left as a gift and permanent installation to be used by the community, continuing to connect them to the concept of Unity of the Earth Mandala.

"The world became my studio. I was a pilgrim who made offerings and gave voice and form to the spirit of the earth and the people I met along the way. I kept expanding the borders of what sculpture was, what art was, integrating it more and more into life itself--the people around me; their problems their hopes, their dreams of the future. I saw that at the root of these problems is the misunderstanding of ourselves as separate, isolated beings needing to exploit the earth and each other for our gain. This dualistic way of thinking is the direct cause of our ecological and social problems which is rapidly leading us toward global disaster."

Vijali Hamilton's second Earth Mandala circling the globe is beginning in Ecuador, the first of nine countries close to the equator. The other countries are Brazil, Nigeria, Somalia, India, Australia, South Pacific Ocean off of Nauru, Kiribati and California, USA. The Earth Mandala is an artistic forum for global understanding and is dedicated to the children of the world. Vijali Hamilton believes that global peace can only arise as the outcome of personal healing through a growing awareness of community and world family. By working through the sacred arts with local artists, performers and community, Vijali Hamilton addresses the people's deepest spiritual, personal and social concerns.

The Guernica Related "NO" Canvas Project in Baghdad

There are many innovative creative projects for peace. The NO project is especially interesting. Baghdad's conceptual Artists Union is working on a project on canvas that aims to capture the immediate consequences of the forthcoming "Shock & Awe" missile attack on Baghdad. Thirty-six inch wide and twenty-yard long rolls of white canvas donated by Conceptual Artist Unions in San Francisco, New York, London, Paris, Berlin and Moscow were recently delivered to Art Centers through out the Iraqi capitol. In the manner of Sol Lewitt[1]'s drawings, the canvas are imprinted with 4 inch square grids the insides of which bear a lavender ink imprint bearing the word "NO." Baghdad artists have taken chalk to measure and prepare both perpendicular and diagonal lines across several of the City's central intersections and Boulevards. When City sirens give advance warning of the attack expected by the middle of this week Conceptual Artist Brigade members will roll out pre-cut canvas strands across the streets while using the chalk lines as their guide. The riveted edges of each canvas will be stretched taut and tied to hook and eye bolts pre-screwed into facing curbs.

The artists will immediately retreat to safety such as it may be found. For the two day duration of the 800 missile attack, possibly most of it at night, the "NO" canvas will receive the full brunt and range of the marks of war and destruction. Flying debris - whether missile or imploding building parts - will variously scar and alter the texture of the canvas, each of which will also absorb the tread marks of military vehicles, tanks and such. No one yet wants to imagine the impact of casualties and remains, such as the marks of blood, the scratch of human hands and the diverse trails and rhythm of footprints.

Project sponsors point out that "These canvas' will represent a different approach than the mythological one of Picasso's Guernicas. For the Western eye the Conceptual Artist Union's work," they say, " is most influenced by the Fifties "Tire Print" work of Robert Rauschenberg and that of the late Ana Mendieta whose blood marked paintings gave performance art its early urgency. Similarly, the sponsors say, "the intention of the "No" canvas' - such as those that may survive and are retrieved - will provide an awesome, if not totally terrifying, rendering of the particulars and horror of this war."

Taken from- After the Fall: Artists for Peace, Justice and Civil Liberties is a fine art gallery and anthology dedicated to peace and justice issues worldwide.

HOW TO BE AN ARTIST FOR PEACE

There are simple steps to making art for peace. You can do it, you do it already. This advice about making art for peace is derived from our work with creativity, spirituality and healthcare at University of Florida College of Nursing and College of Medicine. Mary Rockwood Lane as cofounder and co-director of Arts In Medicine University of Florida developed ways to use creativity to heal patients with life threatening illness. These methods were the subject of her peer reviewed research Spirit Body Healing on how creativity heals with spiritual experience. The process of making art to heal applies to the Caritas peacemaker healing the life threatening illness of war.

RECLAIMING YOUR INNER ARTIST

- Realize you want to be an artist for peace.
- Let go of insecurities. Anyone can do it, we are all artists.
- Let go of fear and your inner critic.
- Say to yourself, "I am an artist for peace."
- Broaden your artistry to include your whole life.
- Realize that being an artist is a natural human ability.

MAKING YOUR LIFE YOUR STUDIO

- Create space in your busy life for creativity for peace.
- Make a commitment to make art for your inner peace and world peace.
- Regard art as an important thing you do to make peace.
- Begin with yourself as the focus of your peacemaking process.
- Make your studio beautiful.
- Put in personal things to make it deeply yours.
- Make it convenient and accessible.
- Create a routine to make art every day.
- Give yourself attention and listen to yourself.
- Create a boundary around yourself
- Create sacred space with a prayer or altar.

CHOOSING A MEDIA

- Don't worry about which media you choose.
- Remember a time when you were most creative as a child. Which media did you use then? Let go of voices from your childhood of criticism, you can do it.
- Which media resonates with your flow of energy?

- Which material comes to your mind first?
- Which process comes to your mind first?
- What is your secret desire?
- Allow yourself to experiment.
- Be open to choices ahead.
- Now, choose one and begin.

How to promote peace with writing

Step one: Starting on the path

- Take time to be with yourself to daydream solutions for peace.
- create a space and a time to write.
- value your writing time like it is gold.
- use a laptop computer, desktop computer, spiral notebook or journal.
- make a notebook your portable studio and take it everywhere.
- write every day, a set amount of time or set number of pages.
- invite your muse, wisdom within or inner Caritas peacemaker to sing to you every day.

Step two: The journey of the creative Caritas peacemaker

- make an intention to promote peace with your writing
- publish, email, write letter to government official
- share your voice, move into community
- speak in public, to schools, churches and amongst friends
- if the whole page intimidates you, write in columns
- it might be easier to write small paragraphs or separate lines
- find colorful pens that delight you

- draw pictures along with the words
- decorate your computer case or journal with beautiful pictures
- When you write let your words flow out
- don't edit or censor, let go of judgment
- write down what you would say to someone in words
- don't worry about making any sense at all (think of Finnegan's Wake by James Joyce)
- feel Her love surrounding you

STEP THREE: DEEPENING

- write every day for peace
- words are powerful
- jot down notes immediately when things come to mind
- bring symbols into your writing
- tell stories to other people out loud
- get into your stories, they will take you "elsewhere"
- have conversations with your characters, invite them to appear
- allow yourself to flow on Her river of words

STEP FOUR: TRANSCENDENCE

- tap into your inner wisdom, your soul's most powerful imagery: put it to words
- poetry is often deeper and closer to the source
- find words in your writing that come up again and again: they are your themes
- love your words and yourself as you read them
- don't be afraid of poetry, you don't have to make it rhyme or have form
- create a support group to read to each other

- bring out deep memories
- write a letter to yourself from your heart
- write a letter to the world from your heart
- let your words take you deep
- make your own life Her living myth
- look for images of light and joy

HOW TO PROMOTE PEACE WITH THE VISUAL ARTS

STEP ONE: STARTING ON THE PATH

- becoming an artist to create Caritas peace, just be creative
- Give yourself time alone to let your images for peace emerge
- Encourage creative ideas for peace strategies to emerge as visual images
- Make posters, flyers, put your work out there
- Your world is your gallery
- start with a sketchbook, pencils and pens
- get a journal for writing and drawing everyday
- make an artist's tote bag that is easy to carry with materials
- buy paints or materials that look like they would be fun to use
- set up a routine to make art every day
- say a prayer for your divine creativity to flow through you for peace

STEP TWO: THE JOURNEY OF THE CREATIVE CARITAS PEACEMAKER

- make an intention to make peace with the visual arts
- release your inner critic, let go of judgment
- keep your appointment with yourself to paint

- collect more materials that would be fun
- make marks or color blotches and play
- set objects that you love around your studio
- find an artist to become a support person
- feel Her love surrounding you

STEP THREE: DEEPENING

- make art for peace everyday
- pay attention to your images of darkness and light, even war and suffering
- let your images of peace or pain emerge without censorship
- respond to the materials that capture your attention
- cultivate a vision of looking at the world
- use a camera to create a visual diary
- allow yourself to be connected to the incredible world of images
- hang your art in your place of work, car, home to transform reality

STEP FOUR: TRANSCENDENCE

- Feel Caritas peace coming through your art
- be compassionate with yourself
- there are no mistakes only opportunities
- experiment with different materials, shapes, and colors
- listen to music while your work to relax
- art is a meditation
- look for images of light and beauty
- you don't have to show it to anyone, its yours

- realize that Her vision is your vision

How to promote Caritas peace with the sacred dance of your life

---

Step one: Starting on the path

- find a space to be your dance floor, where your movement can be free
- allow yourself to stretch to warm up daily
- connect with the energy inside your body
- allow your body to move spontaneously, and follow the movements
- select the music that you love or want to move to
- let the rhythm of life be your music
- transform your ordinary movements to a sacred dance
- walk through your life with the grace of a dancer
- start to dance with explorations in pure movement
- allow the divine dancer to move within you

Step two: The journey of the creative Caritas peacemaker

- see each movement as a deliberate consciousness act
- make an intention to move in beauty and grace
- embody emotions as movements
- use your breath to create an ebb and flow
- use scarves to move air in flowing movements or to simulate water
- access your inner self though dance
- go to the place where emotion merges with movement

- allow sounds to emerge as you dance if that is natural
- be non judgmental, let go of criticism or expectation
- merge with the life-force
- dance to music of the pain and darkness, joy sadness and light
- dance in community with friends and foes

STEP THREE: DEEPENING

- dance within the motions of your day
- draw images and then dance them
- dance symbols
- dance an animal
- dance a tree or rock
- dance an image or a feeling
- move to define space
- go deep inside your body
- if you dance with others make a lot of contact; don't be afraid of appropriate touch
- use imagery in your dance
- dance to connect with your soul

STEP FOUR: TRANSCENDENCE

- visualize your spirit and body becoming one
- feel yourself as a dance of pure light
- allow yourself to fall deeply into the center of a dancing spiral
- allow yourself to dance through life as you move
- receive the energy of the earth
- connect with the dancer in the stars
- honor the mystery of the dance

- dance as one in whirling circles with people in conflict
- create a sacred circle of witnesses to your dance

How to promote Caritas peace with music

Step one: Starting on the path

- find a time each day and listen to music consistently
- pick tapes that you love that resonate with you
- close your eyes and listen
- turn the phones off
- let music take you elsewhere
- breathe with the music
- get in touch with each sound
- return to the pleasure of music
- find a place to sing tone chant
- experience the sounds of nature

Step two: the journey of the creative Caritas peacemaker

- make music an intentional part of peace activities
- play music to relax
- listen to tapes of music that are healing
- bring tapes to any stressful event make your own tape library
- say "no" to hostile or jarring sounds
- go to sound with intention to balance
- become one with the sound
- feel the rhythm in your body
- hum or chant

- sing or repeat words to a rhythm
- sing in the shower
- tone in the shower
- try playing an instrument like a child with joy and without judgment
- start a new instrument
- walk along a stream or brook and listen
- go to the music of the ocean a brook a waterfall and listen
- listen to the wind, to fog
- listen to birds
- feel the harmony of the sound surround you

STEP THREE: DEEPENING

- feel the power rise within you
- allow the vibrational shifts in your body to move through you
- repeat affirmations such as "I am one with my song" to music
- sing a lullaby to yourself or a loved one
- go into the music of your enemy
- invite friends to serenade you with music
- have a friend play the guitar and sing to you
- make your own instrument with things that are around
- use repetitive sound rhythms as an inner chant

STEP FOUR: TRANSCENDENCE

- imagine your spirit soaring as song
- sing to your bones
- sing from your heart
- evoke your God with music and song

- learn sacred chants
- listen to silence
- put yourself in the center of a healing circle of music
- make a drumming circle for healing
- listen to the earth's body sing to you
- turn up the volume of natures healing music
- create a community of music makers
- form singing circles
- let the music carry you to God

GUIDED IMAGERY TO SEE THE WORLD THROUGH THE EYES OF AN ARTIST

Find the special place where you go into your process of meditation and relaxation. Let your relaxation deepen. If you wish you can count your breaths and let your relaxation deepen with each breath.

Now, in your mind's eye, see yourself in a beautiful place. Invite the images of a place you love, a place that is visually and spiritually exciting come to you now. Give yourself time for these images to come. See the place, smell the place, feel the place, hear the place. Now you will see the place anew out of the eyes of the artist. To do this, first say to the place, I love you. If you are on a river, at mountain, a meditation room, say I love you to the place and feel the love flowing from you into the place. If you are in love with a person or a work, feel those feeling now as you love the place you are in.

Now seeing out of the eyes of the lover, look at the colors, hear the sounds, feel the textures of this place. See shadow, light, movement, hear tones, rhythms songs, feel the wind as soft touch of your lover, smell the aroma like a healing herb. Go deeper into the place and look at each detail intently. Look over and over again at one shadow and light, listen intently for one song, one sound. Imagine you are an artist painting the scene, photographing it, writing it as a poem, making the sounds a song, a dance. Concentrate deeply on what you are making as art, see it deeper than you ever have before. See the colors more intensely hear the sounds more intensely, feel the air more intensely.

Now imagine you are with a person who is in conflict with you. He or she can be a family member, an adversary, the enemy. Imagine the person is at peace with you for a moment. In this special moment there in no hostility or threat of violence or anger. Now, breathe deeply and relax. Let the peace that surrounds you flow around the person and you. Now see the person as if you are an artist. See their face, the shadows, the light; see their eyes, their hair, the beauty in their smile. See the beauty in their soul, below their personality. Now go deeper. Imagine the person is filled with love. See the love from above flowing from the person. See light around them, shapes of symbols around them… see their family and loved ones, their babies and grandparents. See the light, the textures, the shapes, the colors, see the beauty; see without judgment.

When you are ready, return to the room where you are doing the exercise and find your grounding. You are back, you can carry the experience of the exercise outward to your life. You will feel stronger and be able to see deeper. You will be in a healing state. Each time you do the exercise you will be more relaxed and be able to go deeper and be more deeply healed.

The next time you go out into nature or are with something you love, do this exercise in the outer world. Notice how the color, sounds, feelings, aroma are more intense after you love or see deeply. This is being there, in the body of your beloved, seeing out of the eyes of the artist.

CHAPTER TEN

CARITAS PROCESS 7. TEACHING PEOPLE TO TRANSFORM TO A NEW FUTURE OF PEACE.

ACTIVELY RECONSTRUCT YOUR OWN FUTURE

Engaging in teaching and learning experiences that honor the other's views is a way to peace. Caritas peacemakers are teachers; they need to be able to meet a person where they are now. They need to understand where the other is to be able to help; they need to know someone is ready for advice, and life change. This is their way of awaking and transforming people's consciousness. The Caritas peacemaker teaches people to move into a new place in their constructed reality for peace. Move into a place where you construct reality yourself, not where you accept a reality made by another and blame them for it. Move past the old construct of war dominance, hatred, imprisonment. It is time for humankind to move past this ancient place of territorial hatred. Move to a new place and reconstruct what does not have integrity. A world based on who is rich and who you know and who has the biggest guns is passé. There is another way. We all know this. The basis of all popular revolutions has been an evanescent glimpse of the new reality over the horizon.

The new future is based on a constructed consensual reality in which people consent only to peace. Peace is achieved through social justice and equality. The changes are real, not talked about, they are from the heart not the head. We start to construct our new reality by defining what we want in the world. If you could design a new world order what would it be? You need to go into your heart, your wisdom place, to find this reality. A positive new way of looking at the world will change people to wage peace. This view needs to come from inside. The media and embedded social organizations will deconstruct as people construct their own reality. The reality constructed by the media and social order is a reality of war, fear, negativity and powerlessness for individuals -especially women and children and people of color. It is still the old reality of mine verses yours, profit and deficit, win and lose. The new feminine reality of nurturing and true democracy of the individual will emerge if we build it together.

People need to be ready to find peace. The Caritas peacemaker finds out if people are ready before teaching.   A true democracy is for the people, not for the leader. When a leader does not follow the people, when a leader does not listen to the voice of the people, it is a totalitarian dictatorship. When a leader does not listen to the voice of the people and says it is because God is for him, it is a religious dictatorship. A democracy is responsible for the safety of the individual people, especially women and children who are now powerless. It needs to protect the individual from violence, especially people of color and people who do not have the economic resources to lobby for power. A democracy run by global companies for their own profit and gain and touted as democracy is false. We all know this. The future will be determined by which path we choose, nurturing or destructive technology. When the government protects the homeland and not the people living in it, it is doing something else, its agenda is self serving, it is protecting the embedded superstructure, not the individual. When women can get raped, children murdered, and poverty and starvation are the order of the day, the people are not protected even if the homeland is safe from terrorism.

Create energy and whirl it into new reality. This reality is yet to be conceived. War as a world event creates a situation where the old reality is taken apart. The war forces us to examine the roots of war. We need to examine the roots of ourselves to deal with peace. We need peace in our own personal life. The greatest struggle for peace is in our daily life. It is with our family, our work, our community. The illusion that you do not construct your own life, that people try to get something from you that they want, must be overturned before world peace can be constructed.

A first step is to restory the world view from uncontrolled patriarchal dominance to a world where the feminine and masculine are in balance and in love. We need to actively make a world where the feminine values of nurturing are honored, expressed, and enhanced as the way of future. The war and world crisis pushes the Caritas peacemaker to look at the non peaceful way, it pushes us to look at our old patterns of being and not take them for granted anymore. It has gone on for too long. We know more than this now. We have moved past this way of being in our hearts and heads. When we make the journey from head to heart the old way of being evaporates and is no longer acceptable. The old way of war conserves energy as an old habit… not dealing with conflict and reacting with war is an old way that is a reflex habit. New ways take energy, creativity and work. To walk a new path takes clearing land; the old path is already clear but it will result in our own and our children's premature deaths. *The Caritas Path to Peace* is active; it takes effort and work to create this new path.

The present path of war and media analysis is cynical, critical, negative… it finds fault in others, it disrespects differences, it has an idealized image of who we are and who the other is. It is waging war on our own humanness; it is like making woman look thin for marketing and profit. It takes effort not to buy into the dominant society's rules. It takes effort to examine and restory and reconstruct reality. What is the story of Saddam and the story of Bush? Listen to their stories and look carefully at their words. What is the story of war? Listen to the generals' stories carefully and look at their words. Look at words of war like "collateral damage". A good way to look at words is through art and poetry. Then look at the story from the other person's point of view to learn something and not criticize. It takes the power of thoughts to deliberately manifest a new reality. Words are powerful; don't be afraid to speak words, they are huge. Words penetrate; thought change the consensual reality. Just as they create a reality with collateral damage we need to create the new reality with our own powerful words.

It is our choice to reconstruct a new reality in our minds and then in the outer world. We can cultivate a place of peacefulness and move into that reality by holding a powerful center of peacefulness within. We can deal with our emotional reactions with critical thought even while we are pushed around and bombarded by intrusions of the media in our place of peace. We can do the impossible, make miracles. Patients are cured of terminal cancer every day. We can dwell in a place of peaceful serenity. We can hold the sacred as the most important place to be. We can hold serenity as the treasure of life. To restory is stopping the old story. To do this we must get in touch with the old story of fear and replace it with a new self created story of love. Stop fear, begin love.

Being awake to negativity and emotional reactions, noticing what comes up from within in conflict is the key. Until we take responsibly for own role in conflict we cannot create world peace. On a personal level, take responsibility for causing your own problems- that requires openness to learning and a lack of defensiveness. When you understand that you are loved, you can be open to learning, take suggestions and not react with the knee jerk of defensiveness and fear. Cultivate serenity, look without attachment, be open and have the expansiveness to embrace that which comes from your inner wisdom place of peace.

TEACHING PEOPLE TO CONCEPTUALIZE AN EMERGING NEW FUTURE

A Caritas peacemaker can help people understand when they are ready:

- You make your own reality- don't blame others.
- Construct a virtual reality of positivity and peace.
- Substitute love for fear.
- You can make a new world acting as an individuals from your own heart and wisdom place.
- Decide as one that the old reality is over.
- Create a new way of reacting to situations with learning, not defensiveness.
- Create peace from equality and social justice.

THE NOOSPHERE AND THE GLOBAL COMMUNITY FOR PEACE

Chardin's view of evolution has much to teach the Caritas peacemaker. He believed that to evolve, matter joined together in ever more complex meetings. Finally compounds joined together to make life. He called life the biosphere, the advancing network of living forms. He believed the biosphere had evolved to the development of human beings. By weaving into a cosmic whole, humans had reached a collective consciousness to become consciousness of themselves. Teilhard says that the destiny of man is to culminate into a consciousness of the species.

The Noosphere

Chardin theorized that the collective consciousness of mankind would ultimately become the "thinking layer of the earth," which he called the *noosphere*. He developed this theory in the early twentieth century. Now in the twenty first century, the noosphere has arrived as the internet and advanced communications.

Chardin theorized that cosmic evolution would not stop with the noosphere. He did not believe the human being was the epitome of evolution; he believed that nature would provide us with another evolutionary opening, " a super-soul above our souls". The whole "gigantic psycho-biological operation" of cosmic evolution points toward a "mega-synthesis" of all the thinking elements of the earth heading towards the realm of the super-human.

Omega point

Teilhard called this super-human place the omega point. It was, for him, the apex of cosmic evolution. He could only imagine what the reality of omega might be like, "a *pure conscious energy*". He described this cosmic energy in the words of a poet. "In the discovery of the sidereal world, so vast that it seems to do away with all proportion between our own being and the dimensions of the cosmos around us, only one reality seems to survive and be capable of succeeding and spanning the infinitesimal and the immense: energy... that floating, universal entity from which all emerges and into which all falls back as into an ocean; energy...the new spirit; energy...the new god.

"In every past generation true seekers, those by vocation or profession, are to be found, but in the past they were no more than a handful of individuals, generally isolated, and of a type that was virtually abnormal. But today...in fields embracing every aspect of physical matter, life and thought, the research workers are to be numbered in the hundreds of thousands, and they no longer work in isolation but in teams endowed with penetrative powers. Research...is in process of becoming a major, indeed the principal, function of humanity." Chardin believed that humanity is "cerebralizing" itself, and slowly but surely building the noosphere, which for him is a "stupendous thinking machine."

THE NEW WORLD ORDER

This step is about readiness for transformation. It not about authoritarian power. It's about liberation of people to give them self knowledge and self control. If there was a new world order based on your work, on your life and beliefs, what would it be? Would it include harmony, a flowing with nature? Would it be like the images from the Greek word for "peace" ("eirene") of a boat sailing on a calm sea? Would it be like a harmony, a song in which all notes and cords blend in perfect agreement or like the reverence for the rhythm of a mother manatee and her baby swimming on a smooth river? We are each connected to a spiritual presence in our life which allows us to feel the wisdom of spiritual traditions and live them. In this time it is not about speaking, but living from the heart.

Would you protect environments and habitats of animals? We each have a spiritual connection in our bodies. We live with compassion... forgiveness in the creative possibilities and infinite creativity of life. There is a creative life force... we are a part of it. The fluidity of our minds, our expansiveness, allows us to think and live in expansive way with room for new thoughts. Internet technology has us all interconnected, interwoven. Would you honor human crafts, what humans touch? One person creates something in world that can be beautiful beyond measure. The spirit of a home or a bowl, reverence for craft is peace.

If you could make a new order filled with life, what would it be… how would you redefine the human value system? Take a moment, do a guided imagery and see if you can glimpse a new reality of peace.

THE RESTORYING TECHNIQUE FOR PEACE

We discovered the restorying method when we watched our patients heal. As they healed, we did the restorying process with them naturally. They started with, "I have cancer and am going to die." The new story that we helped them find was, " I can handle this, I will beat this with the new treatment. I will be the one who is cured. " When the story changed, their lives changed. Suddenly they had hope, positivity, and could act for healing. As we developed the method further, we found the exciting academic research in narrative psychology and post modern theory. This research proved that restorying helped people change their reality. Caritas peacemakers can teach people peace by encouraging them to restory their reality to include peace and peaceful solutions to problems.

Our life is already a story. Each moment we look at the world around us, we see it within a world view. We see ourselves, others, and the situation of war or peace we are in, within a particular view of life or story. Our world view is like a lens that creates our perceptions of reality and in fact creates our reality itself. Our view or attitude about ourselves, our goals, our ability to succeed, creates our future and lets us see and create a reality around us that supports that story. We call your world view or attitude, your story.

What is restorying? You have a story already. It has a past, present, and future. Your story lives within your environment, your friends and your culture. Your story has characters in it, themes, patterns. In your story, in every chapter, there are choices in which you create and manifest your daily moment to moment reality. It is like a theatre that plays out, you are in a role as the character in your story.

What if you want to change you life, what if you want to create world peace? To do this you need to create a new story, to restory you own world view. This strategy will empower you to take action and create a vision of your own life that is who you are and who you want to be. This technique is very powerful. The power of your own word communicates with yourself. It frees your own experience. Everything in your life is a story. We can restory our lives for peace by understanding that a new reality of peace is possible and we can create it in the world. We do not have to do what has been done before - solve conflicts with war or violence. This is the preventive medicine of the future, to conquer violence.

RESTORYING YOUR LIFE EXERCISES

Step one: Finding your present story of peace and war In step one the person gets in touch with the story of peace and war they are living now. To find it all they need to do is look at their life. In this step, the person specifically looks at the words they use and the way the look at things. In this step the person feels their darkness and fear, embodies it, sees who they are now.

Step two: Inviting the new story to appear

The person begins to use new words to describe themselves as a Caritas peacemaker and what is happening. They choose the words carefully to be positive and to show faith in themselves. Next, they choose to look at things with positivity and faith; each time they realize how they looked at something, they choose a new way to see. Finally, the person does a creative process: writes, makes art, volunteers, marches. They invite visionary experiences which inform them of who they are. They experience transformation, a basic restoring takes place that makes their whole life view new. They describe themselves in a new way, they see themselves in a new way and they see themselves loved and cared for.

Step three: Rewriting the story of your life.

The new story emerges in the process, the person sees it, honors it, becomes it, and now tells the new story of who they are. They become the new story. They manifest what they want. They go from fighting a lost cause to being a crucial part of the world and the peacemaking process, a person who helps change reality for everyone.

RESTORING THE PRESENT

It's about mutuality in creating the new present, access to information for liberation. If you are watching a political situation evolve, you can be thinking, "war is here, I couldn't do anything to stop it, I am worthless." Or you can think," the war will stop, peace will come, I will do anything I can for peace. I am powerful, effective, and can change the world." Both these thoughts are a story that shows you who you are and what you think of yourself in the present moment. In each moment there is a story of who you are.

If you have a thought like, "war is inevitable, the rich always win and control the earth", you can choose in that moment to substitute the thought, "people are more together now than ever, eventually we will prevail." The first story will lead to you being sad or helpless, the second story is a meditation to learn empowerment and positivity.

Look at the language in your story and in each moment, rewrite the words in positivity. Look for expectations in the story you hold. If you are expecting war, be the normal situation and get angry, rewrite the story with a new positive expectation. The new story can be, "I will join the collective unity for peace and change the world." Use spiritual ways of looking at yourself to reframe what is happening in the moment.

RESTORYING THE FUTURE

The person's story tells the person a great deal about their future. The story helps make the person's goals clear. To make any decision, a person needs to know his or her priorities. Then he or she can make each choice based on getting what they want. Restorying the future is a way of manifesting the reality you want to live in. Just as you don't know the story before you start the process, you don't know the future. It forms itself around your dreams.

Let's say the reader wants to work for peace. Then, she can make her story the story of the woman who is a Caritas peacemaker in her community. Embellish her story and make it more real. For example, she might say she can lead peace marches, make a website, make a healing circle for peace, put signs up, call neighbors, send email.

RESTORY THE PEACEMAKING PROCESS ITSELF

Affirming, encouraging, following successes are ways that help people discover support systems to change the future externally and internally. That way people can create the best solutions for peace. The Caritas peacemaker helps people create a story of hope. Create a story of a miracle. Create a story where the person is empowered to act and change his/her life. The physician heals by treating with drugs and surgery, by inspiring confidence and reassuring the patient that they will heal them. They say, "I am the expert; follow me and I will take you there." They create a new story from the old. From the story "I am incurable," they say, "I am the first doctor who can heal you, do this and you will be cured." The patient then has a new story: "I will be healed by this new physician." You can be a Caritas peacemaker with hope to change the world. You can make yourself the one who can do it. You can be the miracle maker.

The world needs you

Make your life meaningful. The basic myth we learned from our patients is that life becomes rich when you contribute to the whole. Our patients taught us that if you believe that without you the world would not be as good, you will feel valued and powerful.

Making meaning

Carl Jung tells this story of living a life within a story of meaning.

> Jung was in New Mexico visiting a Taos pueblo. Ochiwa Biano, the chief of the Taos Indians, stood on the roof of the pueblo at sunrise and pointed to the sun. He told Jung, "without my people, without our prayers, the sun would not rise in the morning and the world would be dark." Jung said that modern humans have lost this connection with nature and lost the personal stories which give their life real meaning. He suggested that finding a new story to live by would be deeply healing for people today.

In our research, we learned that as part of their healing and restoring of their lives, people acted in a way they believed was helping the world. Much of their new story was based on generosity, giving… they were proud and spiritually strong. They received gifts of spirit in their visions and shared the gifts with others. This part of changing your story is about going out in the world, from a place of personal power, to make difference in world. The people feel empowered with action, not belief, not by words, but by doing. It is not about sitting in your room worrying, it is about entering into life's fray, taking sides, and making change. To make world peace come you have to write letters, go to meetings, protest, join organizations, raise money and act. If you believe that peace needs to be, you have meaning in your new story.

CHAPTER ELEVEN

CARITAS PROCESS 8. VISIONING HEALING ENVIRONMENTS FOR WORLD PEACE

Healing environments for peace include basic comfort, removing toxic stimuli, dealing with cold, hunger, and noise. Healing environments for peace also include therapeutic touch, massage, and love. Dealing with poverty, pollution, ugliness, the destruction of nature…these are crucial to prevent war. Protecting people from war and violence is about basic safety. War is an ultimate destruction of environment, of dignity, autonomy, and aesthetic surroundings. War and violence is the opposite of treating the environment as sacred. Indigenous cultures looked at the world, its animals and plants, the earth as sacred, as our mother. Now, creating sacred space is a first step to creating our environment for peace.

CREATING SACRED SPACE

MY PATIENT'S ROOM IS A TEMPLE: A STORY.

She was tall and elegant, an African American woman who exuded quiet confidence and power. She was a young doctor, just finished with her training at Stanford University in internal medicine and then oncology. She was attending a conference on alternative cancer care and we could see her interest in my presentation. She took us aside at a break and told us this story:

> "When I see a patient with cancer, I have a ritual I do." She stopped. I could see that she was embarrassed, which was unusual for her, and hesitant to go on. I told her it was all right, I was used to these kinds of stories, so she continued. "As I walk up to the patient's room. I pause. And then everything changes. I go into the place in my world where I am in perfect peace, I go into the stillness, the silence, into the place where I have gone to pray since I have been a little girl. Time and space change all around me. Then, there is a silence and a quality of light, a grayness a radiance from within itself that is so beautiful that it takes me completely and washes me and prepares me and purifies me.

"In that moment, pregnant with peace, I fill it, I pray, I give thanks to God for allowing me to be a physician, for my abilities, for this opportunity to heal. I ask God to come with me into the patient's room and to be with me and give me insight, healing power, and strength. I ask for the ability to heal, to listen and to love. And then in my mind's eye, I picture the patient's room as a sacred temple. I picture columns on each side of the door like in a Greek healing temple. I picture owls on each column for the healing Goddess Athena.

"Then I drop deeper into my center, my spiritual place of healing and I go into the room. Inside the room, I am just me, I am the physician I have been trained to be, I do the best I can with my skills but-- I am more. I have God with me helping me,; I see the patient with God's love and I see me with God's love too. I am able to listen and be fully present. In this altered state I can see things and hear things and get ideas that I don't usually get. I get ideas, see colors and light… I am so alive. In the room, I am an ordinary physician and a special one too. Does that make sense to you? Is that what you mean in your presentation: Shaman Medicine ?"

This chapter is about the Caritas peacemaker making the environment and the space he or she works in sacred. It is about creating a space that is full of power and energy. It is about giving thanks and using prayer, calling in helpers, guides, angels, God, Creator, to help you in the healing process.

PRAYER CREATES SACRED SPACE.

Many healers all over the world, no matter what tradition they are trained in, do a prayer to bring in the spiritual forces they work with. Healing work undertaken with prayer to a higher force gains power and strength. The Caritas peacemaker can enhance sacred space by giving thanks in intentional prayer. Caritas healing includes all spiritualities, all religions; prayer and going inward to the meditative state can be done by anyone. The Caritas peacemaker can give thanks, ask for guidance, and pray. This can be your prayer for our work to be healing to ourselves, others, and the earth.

A PRAYER FOR CARITAS PEACE

As we start on our work for Caritas peace, let us pray, honoring all those who help us on the way. We call for all religions, all traditions, all countries, to stand together with us in this sacred work. We honor all manifestations of spirit, God, Goddess, Buddha, and all wisdom Teachers, to help us with this work. As we pause, we pray for peace on earth, peace in ourselves and in our relationships, peace for families, peace in the communities we work in. We pray for peace to evolve to a Caritas consciousness. Give us the power to live with caring actions. Help us receive the wisdom that will inform us on this journey. Caritas is a way of being and a way of praying. We pray for peace, may we move forward in peace.

CHARACTERISTICS OF SACRED SPACE

Sacred space is visionary space, it is non-ordinary reality. It is space that is full of meaning, pregnant with power. It is space that has similar characteristics so that each practitioner who goes into it usually does similar things. Sacred space itself calls the Caritas peacemakers and tells them what to do. The ritual is dictated from the space, not the space from the ritual.

Characteristics of sacred space

- It involves gratitude and blessings. It starts with giving thanks.
- It may have an altar, a place to put sacred personal objects.
- It often involves fire, a candle, sage, incense.
- It always involves a prayer to a higher force, God, The Creator, Great Spirit.
- It involves offerings different for each culture.

- It often acknowledges the four directions or up for heaven and down for underworld.
- It often involves helpers or guides who are invited to come- God, Great Spirit, angels, spirit guides, spirit animals, nature forces.

In sacred space the Caritas peacemakers feel their own oneness with the earth. The environment is comfortable... you, and the person you are working with are comfortable. This creates confidence for both. In sacred space you work to change the environment to be one of harmony, peace and beauty. You deal with light and color, you care about detail, you put work into it. You do this with intention. What goes in is what comes out. Sacred space in the physical world is clean fresh air, clean water, beauty... it reflects the inner sacred space within you.

HOW TO CREATE SACRED SPACE WITHIN YOUR BODY

Sacred space is created from within and from without. To create sacred space from within, you create it within your own body. You body is your temple, your doorway to enter into sacred space. The first step in creating sacred space in your body is to become aware of your breathing. You do this by taking slow breaths in and out... you convert your breathing to abdominal breathing, centered in your belly, grounded in your body. You allow your body to fill up with light as you breathe... this helps you to open. You open up the top of your head and allow an axis to form that connects you with the earth. The axis goes through you from the earth, up through your body, up out of your head, to the sky. It connects mother earth to father sky through the sacred body. It allows the energy of the earth to go through your head... it allows a flow though you from the universal energy of creation and healing.

As you move, as you breathe, Caritas love, light and healing energy come through you. You do not use your own energy; the univer- sal energy moves through you. It does it itself... something comes through, you tap into the eternal wellspring of Caritas energy that flows through all things. This creates spaciousness inside of you, you expand. The sacred space allows you to find a reverence in the detail of the present moment, a reverence in looking at the other. As you look at the way their mouth is, their lips are, the way their eyes move, as you see the little details about their body, you absorb the unique and special beauty of that person.

As you slow down your breathing, you allow yourself a moment to be in sacred place. You do that with intent. Every moment in sacred space exists in a transient flash; time slows down... in that moment relish it, observe it, be awake to it. Be awake to how you move though space and time, be directed, focused and soft. You can do it, you are moving fluidly. In visionary space you can move with grace... with practice you can move and have grace. In grace you see yourself and the other illuminated. You actually create a sacred altar within your self and the other. You do this with prayer, you allow your activities to be your offering. What you offer is your life. Awareness of being you is the beginning of your sacred place.

AN EXERCISE TO CREATE SACRED SPACE IN YOUR BODY

Make yourself comfortable. You can be sitting down or lying down. Loosen tight clothing, uncross your legs and arms. Close your eyes. Let your breathing slow down. Take several deep breaths. Let your abdomen rise as you breathe in, and fall as you let your deep breath out. As you breathe in and out you will become more and more relaxed. You may feel feelings of tingling, buzzing, or relaxation; if you do, let those feelings increase. You may feel heaviness or lightness... you may feel your boundaries loosening and your edges softening.

Now as you breathe in, let you body expand. As you breathe out, let it stay in the larger state. As you expand, you can feel energy and see light between your cells. The new space created in the expansion fills with God's energy and light with each breath. Feel the energy, feel the buzzing, the vibration, the movement increase with each breath.

If it is comfortable for you, let your boundaries diffuse a little bit. Let them become softer, more open. Let the love and light of the earth around you come into you, let your love and light go outwards those around you and heal.

SEEING YOURSELF AS A GIFT

As a Caritas peacemaker you are the gift. In your mind, you see that you are a gift to the other to heal them. You realize that your education and training and Caritas ability are gifts to you that you offer the other. By being who you are, you have a source of Caritas energy that flows from you. Your body is a Caritas environment that holds spirit. Your body is the temple of your soul… your mind is too… your emotions are your tools to heal. Honor this aspect of yourself that allows you to see in the other. All the work you have done and all the work you do is your gift to the world.

THE CARITAS EMBODIMENT OF SPIRIT

Your body is the place from which you care. Your own voice resonates with the echo of a loving universe. You are in harmony with God's breath. Experience spaciousness, become large. Experience oneness, call forth a direction with intention. Within a void filled with requests, manifest a reality as if you are in harmony with life. This resonates with essence down to the level of the purest spirit. It is a pureness through which you can vibrate the energy of essence on anything. Sacred space in the microcosm is the place in which electrons spin together around the nucleus. The movement of electrons in space is sacred space. It is open and expanded. What you do in it creates or destroys the universe; it is huge and full in intention. It is the place of power, of manifestation, of the universe being born and destroyed.

PREPARATION OF THE PHYSICAL SPACE

Preparation of physical sacred space involves your own ritual structure; it depends on your own traditions and teachers. It involves setting up the room… the details are different for each person, but the themes of preparation with intent are the same. It can be washing hands for a surgeon, lighting incense in a room for a massage therapist, or playing music for a woman at home with a sick child.

Many healers start before the person comes to them. Some begin the morning of a treatment, others even the night before. They sleep on it… in their sleep they tune in on what they need, where they are, what their function is in helping the other. They ask, "what can I add, how can I help?" The answer comes as visual and kinesthetic information. It is larger than their body. They say things… they ask for cleansing, for healing, for help moving energy… they make use of the whole environment for healing with intent and making sacred space.

HAND WASHING AS RITUAL

Hand washing is ritual, it creates sacred space where you create an opportunity to use the healing qualities of water to purify yourself and start anew. You cleanse yourself to create another experience with another human being. It's an intimate ritual that allows taking a pause, reflecting, and letting go. It can be seen as a ritual to ask yourself for purification and change… the act is a preparation to visualize healing, to ask for cleaning, moving, energy. It is an act for transforming your own hands into healing tools for the work you will do. Hands are sacred objects to touch the body of another human being for healing.

GETTING DRESSED IS SACRED CEREMONY.

Getting dressed, adorning yourself, is making yourself ready to move; it is the beginning of your transition from being at home to being in your sacred work environment. Getting dressed with intent is an act to embody and create an energy field where you are healing the environment. The body is your healing environment, your clothing is part of your healing environment. How you attend to own nature is creating an environment for healing… your odor, hair, hygiene, interfaces with the other human's energy field. Intentionally adorn yourself with clothing to prepare to do sacred work.. Choose objects that are meaningful to remind you of healing power; objects can be power objects for healing.

POWER OBJECTS

A body worker describes his way of preparing sacred space before a session:

> "The most important act begins before I enter the patient's room. I see the doorway as a threshold. Before I enter, for a moment I pause. I thank the person for coming to me and having faith in me to be able to heal them. I thank them for opening themselves up to me so can heal. I express gratitude in my own mind for being able to do this work, and gratitude for the person for coming. I clear my own mind of thoughts and concerns. I go into a place where I am only with what is happening in the next moment and what they came for. I create a space where I am open like a bowl that will receive anything they say and be with them. I do not think a certain way. It is a protective time in the room with them, only them and me and the spirit."

Another healer told us:

> " I raise my energy level as I am going in the door. I am aware of being within light and tuning into it. It is a conscious decision, then everything gets brighter. The healing light I see comes from the center of everything, we are a part of it. As I walk in, I am conscious of the change of energy in that room. When I think about the person I work with, I say a prayer and hold space. I ask myself,

'What do they need, What can I do?' and then I feel it. I tune into people, I make myself available. They take what they need. I consciously make myself available so they can get it. That is who I am all the time. I don't think, they flash in. It is intuitive, it comes in; then I know they need something. I feel, I am light, I am giving them light. I am giving someone that essence, letting them take that essence from the universe through me as a shamanic healer."

TRADITIONAL SACRED SPACE: SAGE AND CEDAR

Native Americans give offerings to the Creator and use medicines like sage and cedar to prepare sacred space. Plants like sage or cedar are believed to come from Creator to help humans heal. The plant is used to embody the power the Creator placed in the physical world. Each culture has a story of how the sacred medicines came to them from the Creator. When the medicine is used in a ceremony, the sacred gift is reenacted and embodied.

How to sage a space.

To begin a healing, or to begin any ritual or ceremony, we burn aromatic sage or cedar bundles to cleanse the site and remove impurities. Sage has traditionally been used by first nations peoples for centuries. You can sage the room or even the entire house, if you wish. We burn the sage in an abalone shell or special sage burner. Light the sage and push its rising smoke to the edges of the room with a feather or with your hand. Wave the sage in a clockwise spiral and the house will feel different afterwards. You can use many varieties of sage, cedar and herbs to create sacred space. As you sage, say prayers, picture cleansing, thank the creator, whatever comes to you. What you feel in your heart as you sage, is what is important. Do it with intention, with prayer, with peace.

TOBACCO OFFERING

Traditional Native American shaman are given an offering of tobacco by the patient before a healing. It is ceremonial to bring an offering out of respect and honor before the healing, to offer the Creator. Some healers will not take money; the tobacco offering is the only payment. Michael Samuels has never taken money from a patient since he graduated medical school. His teacher Rolling Thunder taught him that in Native American tradition, a healer did not take money for sacred work. He believed him and has used that as a way to heal ever since.

Guided imagery: creating sacred space

Make yourself comfortable and start your process to go into a meditative, receptive state. Let these feelings of relaxation spread throughout your body. Let your relaxation deepen. If you wish you can count your breaths and let your relaxation deepen with each breath.

In your mind's eye picture the place where you do your healing work. It can be your office, a hospital room, an operating room, a place outdoors, anywhere you have been or imagine you could be to heal. Before you enter that space, pause a moment and say a prayer. Ask the power you believe in to help you make the space you heal in sacred space. Give thanks to the creator for this healing moment, for your ability to heal and help someone. Now in your mind's eye see the space becoming sacred. Call in helpers, guides, spirit animals, teachers, to be with you in this healing work. Call in the Creator to be with you in this healing work. Now imagine the space you are in is filling with light, imagine the space is becoming brighter and brighter. Imagine that angels and helpers have come to the person you are working with to help them.

Now you can picture the space changing physically. You can imagine an altar, sacred art, sage, Native American art, Christian art, Buddhist art, whatever votives would make the space sacred for your own personal healing work. See what comes to you as you invite the space to change physically and become sacred. You can picture candles, incense, a medicine wheel, paintings or sculpture, things you have found, objects from nature, bones, feathers, rocks. Now you can imagine the place is painted and decorated in a sacred way... you can even imagine its shape changing to round, the lighting changing, the sounds changing. Allow yourself to design your own sacred healing space, even through it may not happen in the outer world immediately. This space is in your virtual reality, in your mind, and is in resonance in the outer world. Now enter the space and begin your healing.

When you are ready, return to the room where you are doing the exercise and do your grounding re-entry work. Now open your eyes. Look around you. Stand up and stretch, move your body, feel it move. You are back; you can carry the experience of the exercise outward to your life. You will feel stronger and be able to see deeper. You will be in a healing state. Each time you do the exercise you will be more relaxed and be able to go deeper and be more deeply healed.

PHYSICAL ENVIRONMENTS IN HOSPITALS AS HEALING

Health futurist Lee Kaiser talks about the convergence of Gnosis and the Arts

"An amazing and highly productive convergence is taking place among science, spirituality, the arts, and healing. This convergence is reorganizing the way we deliver health services and will greatly accelerate human evolution.

We need to get together and share our collective awareness as artists, designers, and healers. We need to explore new dimensions of aesthetic consciousness. We need to design potent human environments that heal disease and promote human health and wellbeing.

"Aesthetics is design. A profound appreciation for aesthetics is characteristic of heightened consciousness. Aesthetics is one of the pathways to spiritual enlightenment. It stimulates high frequency emotional, mental, and spiritual energies. It increases the vibratory rate of the soul and in so doing, invokes healing holograms that have the power to reorder disordered systems in the physical body. The healing arts can restore mind/body functions as dramatically as drugs and surgery. Artistic healing interventions are simply modalities that utilize energies from the higher dimensions, namely the fourth, fifth, sixth, and seventh dimensions. Today, most of scientific medicine is focused in the third dimension. This is the domain of modern science where physical cures take place. Healing, by contrast, is a spiritual intervention and requires a higher dimension. Of course, what is needed is a multidimensional approach – a convergence of scientific medicine and spiritual healing via ` art. This convergence, which is now beginning, will make miracles commonplace in our healthcare institutions.

"In the fourth dimension, transformational art forms trigger emotional energies and stimulate swirling astral currents. In the fifth dimension, they dissolve stagnant thought forms and create new mental matrices. In the sixth dimension, they coalesce soul substance and build a bridge of subtle matter between soul and Spirit. In the seventh dimension, transformational art forms express themselves as new spectrum rainbow colors with the accompanying music of the spheres. In the seventh dimension, everything is an art form. Everything sounds its note and radiates its color. This is the ultimate aesthetic dimension. It is sometimes glimpsed by people as they pass through the near-death or near-birth states. Such a glimpse is always a life-changing event of monumental proportions. In the seventh dimension, art is life and life is art. There is no separation between the two.

"Healing changes can be initiated in any of the higher dimensions. The changes occur as a result of resonance between inner qualities of consciousness and outer artistic forms created from dimensional substance. Transformational art resonates with a person's dimensional vehicles. It evokes a subtle response that feeds down and induces a greater coherence in the lower vehicles, including the mind/body vehicle that resides in the third dimension. The higher coherence has healing properties. It is often evidenced as increased production of alpha, theta, and delta brain waves. Numerous studies have shown that greater brain coherence is associated with healing.

"Human consciousness is shaped by the space it occupies. Therefore, a design for space is a design for consciousness. The isomorphism between consciousness and space permits us to design healing environments in hospitals and clinics. Every physical space contains an encoded message. Modern hospital rooms broadcast the message, 'we will take care of you.' A better message might be, 'this is a nurturing space where you are able to heal yourself.'

"Buildings heal. Trees and plants heal. Water heals. Music heals. Art heals. Color heals. Sound heals. Texture heals. Fragrance heals. And of course, doctors, nurses, and other caregivers heal. Why not orchestrate all of these agents of healing in a coordinated effort? Such will be the future of healthcare as art, spirituality, and healing converge.

"As we probe the fruitful convergence of aesthetics and healing, we will encounter some exciting frontier areas like: (1) using sound and images to resonate with a patient's spiritual DNA, thereby reactivating hereditary disease patterns and clearing them, (2) connecting the patient's neurological system to art, generating devices that are responsive to training and biofeedback, (3) using sound and color to facilitate passage to higher dimensions in conscious deathing, or (4) using powerful art forms to connect with the patient's archetypes and empower his personal healing mythology.

"There is no limit to where our imagination, creativity, and courage can take us. Life is ultimately a waking dream. It is an art form of our own construction. All we have to do is look up, to perceive the possibilities that exist beyond our three-dimensional box.

"What is art? Is it the picture hanging upon the wall, the wall upon which the picture hangs, the building in which it is placed, the land upon which it resides or the planet where it is located? The answer is a resounding 'yes.' Does the picture reside in the third, fourth, fifth, sixth, or seventh dimension? Again the answer is a resounding 'yes'. With these two 'yeses', we move into the realm of deep aesthetics. In the last analysis, the provision of healthcare may be nothing but a special application of deep aesthetics where the disharmony of disease is transmuted into the deep harmony of the music of the spheres."

HOW TO MANIFEST PEACE WITH YOUR BODY

1. Your body is your sacred space, your personal environment to be an instrument to manifest peace.

2. In this body you can tap into an energetic field within yourself that is a communion of human physical and spiritual energy to manifest an energetic field for peace.

3. When you do this as a human beings, you are in unity oneness , when one body becomes energized , you take the embodiment of the Caritas energetic field for peace and you project it like a laser to extend it and to create an energy field of the whole group of Caritas peacemakers for peace.

What are environments for peace? They are temples, churches, nature, ancient monuments like Stonehenge, Delos, where are places people pilgrimage for peace? You can see this is on sites like:

Pilgrimage for peace

Places Hiroshima

http://www.peacepilgrim.org/links1.htm

All over the earth people are pilgrimaging for peace to sacred sites, as healing acts

SACRED SPACE AND ENVIRONMENTS: TEMPLES AND WATER

Community is the opposite of war-- war separates and fractions, community defeats war. There are inexhaustible techniques to cause war, and also to cause peace. For techniques to make peace, we can look at nature, flow, oneness, creatures in ecosystems in balance together... we can learn from the environment of living creative life, exploring possibilities with community.

Caritas peacemakers for Peace bring together energy. They can help create healing environments, healing water, healing air pollution, healing community. Florence Nightingale talked about healing environments, about sanitation, light, air. She founded the profession of nursing and dealt with many environmental issues caused by war. Her basic environmental actions were bringing in air and light, sanitation and basic water cleanliness. She advised people to go into nature, enjoy trees, use color... she was an ecologist nurse activist. All caritas peacemakers have to become environmentalists and advocates for peace, to save the environment. Now, when caritas peacemakers create environmental changes, it changes consciousness to create peace.

Create caring healing spaces- create Psycho {IS THIS THE RIGHT WORD???} architectural spaces, create sacred geometry, create beautiful art nature spaces... build waterfalls in hospitals; this changes consciousness. Draw on symbols and archetypes for spiritual change, tap into sacred unconscious, reunite with other cultures to share the meaning found in diverse cultures. Ancient sites shared the experience of humanity; the pilgrimage was a common denominator in the history of the world- it happened to humanity.

Caritas peacemakers for Peace can use physics to enhance healing power in sacred sties to harness the vortex of energy for peace. They can use harmony and wholeness in the environment to create peace. Go to Hiroshima or Jerusalem; create sacred stories and events that heal yourself and heal humanity.

PERENNIAL WISDOM, ENVIRONMENTS AND PEACE

Lee Kaiser speaks of The Perennial Wisdom. He says that, "The term perennial wisdom refers to the collective wisdom of humankind since the beginning of life on Planet Earth. It has come down through the ages in various religions, traditions, and schools of philosophy. The perennial wisdom studies "what is." It seeks to understand the structure and operation of the cosmos. It is interested in discovering and applying spiritual laws in our material dimension.

"IF YOU STUDY THE PERENNIAL WISDOM YOU WILL BE ABLE TO FIND YOUR INDIVIDUAL PLACE IN THE OVERALL SCHEME OF THINGS. IT IS ALSO THE MISSING INGREDIENT IN HEALTHCARE TODAY. IF APPLIED, IT WOULD SOLVE MANY OF OUR CONTEMPORARY HEALTHCARE ISSUES NOW POSING AS ECONOMIC, POLITICAL, SOCIAL, AND ETHNIC PROBLEMS.

"Roots of the perennial wisdom include: tribal shamanism, the Hermetic Tradition, alchemy, esoteric Christianity, the Jerusalem Church, the Essenes, the Cathars, the cathedral builders, the Druids, the Bards, the Greek mysteries, the grail legends, paganism, Sophia, Jewish Kabbalah, and Knights Templar. In other words, the tradition is scattered throughout the spiritual literature of the world. It is illustrated in the Tarot. It is symbolically depicted in the sacred geometry of the pyramids, the cathedrals, and chapels like Rosslyn."

THE CARITAS PEACEMAKER HAS VISIONS THAT INFORM HER ABOUT WHAT TO DO

Healing environments for the physical and spiritual self that respect basic human dignity are how we change our world. Look for the visions that inform your life. Look for Her vision; she is the Goddess… her hand is peace, holding, nurturing, filled with light. Around her is the light, around her are the flames and the doves, blue and golden.

She is surrounded by energy; she is a powerful woman and healer. Becoming Her is your job; she can merge with another to see.

To find the visions that inform your life, go to nature, make art, go deep inward into the visionary world. Then, look for messages. You can recognize the nuggets of gold that give you the crucial visions of your life by paying attention to your body feelings. Bear witness to your own visions; that is a powerful act. To bear witness is to receive the story, to honor the visions and their energy by looking at them closely. Restory, create meaning, bear witness to your own life. The visions you have are your creative ideas, they are you channeling spirit. The connection between you and spirit gives you power and strength.

Marianne Williamson said,

"Our deepest fear is not that we are inadequate.
Our deepest fear is that we are powerful beyond measure.
It is our light, not our darkness, that most frightens us.
We ask ourselves,
"Who am I to be brilliant, gorgeous, talented, fabulous?'
Actually,
Who are you not to be?
You are a child of God.
Your playing small doesn't serve the world.
There's nothing enlightened about shrinking,
So that other people won't feel insecure around you.
We were born to make manifest the Glory of God that is within us.
It's not just in some of us, it's in EVERYONE.
And as we let our own light shine,
We unconsciously give others permission to do the same.
As we are liberated from our own fear,
Our presence automatically liberates others."

When you come into place of the Caritas peacemaker, you leave yourself behind and you speak through another voice. It's Her voice or His voice that you speak though. When I lecture, I get into a place where I tune into a frequency in my chest -I am very relaxed. I almost experience an altered state of consciousness, I get very large. In that moment I am hovering within myself, and someone else stands up in me and begins to speak. I can hear Her voice, She is speaking. If I get out of Her way, a voice speaks through me, it is a voice of tremendous confidence- She radiates - that's the voice of the Caritas peacemaker.

INTUITION

Anyone can benefit by building their intuitive tools. The realization or hunch, the place in the gut of knowing the truth beneath words, is useful to any Caritas peacemaker. The Caritas peacemaker needs to be an expert in intuitive reasoning. The Caritas peacemaker needs to know inside herself what is wrong in a situation and how to fix it. It is like a psychic ability, it is a way of seeing. All healers do this to some extent. Physicians tell us they had a hunch, they knew something was wrong, they knew where to look to find the problem. You can use your intuition for people and problem solving to make peace.

The Caritas peacemaker is an expert in seeing a conflict situation with compassion and love. This way of seeing enables them to act without judgment and to find a solution to conflict. When the enemy is seen with love, he sees himself with love. When the enemy is seen with love, the universal forces of love come to him and make peace. The Caritas peacemaker can see out of eyes of the enemy, and thus bear witness to someone else's life. This helps them hold the place for compassion and love. Intuition and visioning include seeing out of the eyes of your adversary.

DEEPENING YOUR GUIDED IMAGERY EXPERIENCE

The guided imagery exercises that preceded this chapter have allowed you to get used to guided imagery as a process. In this chapter you can deepen the process and improve your ability to image and get ideas for peace. Psychologists divide imagery into several categories. Memory images are evoked by events that took place in the past; imagination images are not based on discrete events from the outer world- they are the result of combining the memories of events in new and creative ways. Some psychologists believe imagination images come from outside us, from the world of the spirit. Dream images are experienced in sleep, hypnopompic images are the visions we see as we awaken, hypnagogic images the images we see while falling asleep. Visions are images experienced while awake or in a trance that are very vivid. Hallucinations are images experienced while awake that are poorly controllable. "Vividness" and "controllability" are terms that show us how psychologists describe the imagery experience. When the experience of imagery is intense, when the images are bright, loud, or very attention getting, they are "vivid." When images are unbidden, cannot be gotten rid of, or cannot be changed, they are "poorly controllable."

In his book, Seeing With The Mind's Eye, Michael divided imagery into two basic types- receptive and programmed. Receptive imagery comes to you, it arrives on the scene, bidden or unbidden, and rests in your mind's eye. Programmed imagery is different. You choose an image and hold it in your thoughts for a reason. The choice may be deliberate or you may choose an image that came to you from the receptive space. The more you do guided imagery exercises, the more you can receive images as creative ideas to inform your life. The Caritas peacemaker can use images and visions as the source of inspiration for creative problem solving and for holding prayers of peace to manifest them in reality.

A DEEPER GUIDED IMAGERY FOR PEACE

Make yourself comfortable. You can be sitting down or lying down. Loosen tight clothing, uncross your legs and arms. Close your eyes. Let your breathing slow down. Take several deep breaths. Let your abdomen rise as you breathe in, and fall as you let your deep breath out.

As you breathe in and out you will become more and more relaxed. You may feel feelings of tingling, buzzing, or relaxation; if you do, let those feelings increase. You may feel heaviness or lightness; you may feel your boundaries loosening and your edges softening.

Now let yourself relax. Let your feet relax, let your legs relax. Let the feelings of relaxation spread upwards to your thighs and pelvis. Let your pelvis open and relax. Now let your abdomen relax, let your belly expand, do not hold it in anymore. Now let your chest relax; let your heartbeat and breathing take place by themselves. Let your arms relax, your hands relax. Now let your neck relax, your head, your face. Let your eyes relax, see a horizon and blackness for a moment., let these feelings of relaxation spread throughout your body. Let your relaxation deepen. If you wish you can count your breaths and let your relaxation deepen with each breath.

In your mind's eye, picture your bedroom. Look around this familiar place, see its shape and size, where the windows are, where the door-way is. See its furniture, your bed, chairs, dressers. See paintings on the wall, sculpture, things you love. Smell its special aroma, feel the bedspread with your hands. Be there; use all your senses to make it real. This is a memory image, an image from your memory of what exists in the outer world.

Now you will change it and turn the memory image into an imagi-nation image. Let the shape of your room change. Let it get larger, round or square, let its ceiling height change. Let your bed rise and float up like it is weightless. Let the windows get larger; put in plants, art, water fountains, the outdoors; let the light change; see stars, the moon through beautiful skylights. Allow your own bedroom to be a mystical place of great beauty and love, a peaceful garden in your life.

Now bring in the energy of peace. In your mind's eye imagine your guides, teachers, helpers, are above sending peaceful energy to you. Imagine the stars above and earth below send peaceful energy in to you. Let it come down from above like a soft rain or like stardust. Let it come up from below like the earth's touch, like dew, like a rising mist.

Let this energy of peace from the creator and from the sky and earth heal you deeply. Let it rise up into you, wash you, energize you and give you peace.

Now you can imagine you are with another person. In your mind's eye see the energy of peace that has come into you go into the person you are with. You can picture a family member, a friend, an associate, or an adversary. Now see a light in your heart. Imagine the light going from your heart to their heart. See your heart opening, see their heart opening, receiving the light. Let this image change; see how your own energy of peace flows from you to them. Let the light come from above into you. Let the light come from a teacher or sacred figure to you. See the light coming from the heart of the sacred figure above you into your heart, and then into the person you are with.

When you are ready, return to the room where you are doing the exercise. First move your feet and then move your hands. Move them around and experience the feeling of the movement. Press your feet down onto the floor, feel the grounding, feel the pressure on the bottom of your feet, feel the solidity of the earth. Feel your backside on the chair; feel your weight pressing downwards. Now open your eyes. Look around you. Stand up and stretch, move your body, feel it move. You are back; you can carry the experience of the exercise outward to your life. You will feel stronger and be able to see deeper. You will be in a healing state. Each time you do the exercise you will be more relaxed and be able to go deeper and be more deeply immersed in the energy of peace.

A GUIDED IMAGERY TO SEE YOUR WORK AS A CARITAS PEACEMAKER

Make yourself comfortable And go through your process of relaxation and receptivity.

Let your relaxation deepen. If you wish you can count your breaths and let your relaxation deepen with each breath.

Now, in your mind's eye see yourself in your most creative space. Let yourself be without limits, totally free. Imagine that you could do anything you want to for world peace. You can meet with the President, the leader of the U.N.; you can dream, touch, fly. You can chant, sing, dance, move healing energy, pray, talk to Jesus, stop war with your mind, anything you want to do. You can be a lawyer, a diplomat, an activist, peace artist, a poet, a mask maker, a dancer, a priest, anything. It is all possible, it is all true. For this guided imagery, let yourself dream.

Now see yourself working for peace in the work you imagine. See yourself meeting, doing ceremony, making a website, teaching, making art, traveling… anything you can dream can become real.

When you are ready, return to the room where you are doing the exercise. First move your feet and then move your hands. Move them around and experience the feeling of the movement. Press your feet down onto the floor, feel the grounding, feel the pressure on the bottom of your feet, feel the solidity of the earth. Feel your backside on the chair; feel your weight pressing downwards. Now open your eyes. Look around you. Stand up and stretch, move your body, feel it move. You are back; you can carry the experience of the exercise outward to your life. You will feel stronger and be able to see deeper. You will be in a healing state. Each time you do the exercise you will be more relaxed and be able to go deeper and be more deeply healed.

A WALK THOUGH WOODS FOR PEACE

A walk In nature is wonderful place to see and listen and get ideas for peace. Visions come during a walk; creative people use walks in nature to get ideas for art, inventions, science and music. Take a walk; let yourself listen to a waterfall. Develop your ability to enter visionary space. As you walk let yourself go deep, into the sounds, smells, feelings. How does the wind feel on your face? How does the earth feel under your feet? Let what you see take you into your inner world. Allow emotions to come to the surface. Allow dreams and visions to appear, listen to the animals, birds, insects… let them speak to you about peace in inner voices and visions. Ask the springs to talk about peace, ask the mountain, ask the forest, ask the earth. Then listen to what you hear in the thoughts of your mind.

A GUIDED IMAGERY TO BE IN NATURE

Make yourself comfortable and go into your relaxation and meditation process.

Let your heartbeat and breathing take place by themselves. As your relax, let your eyes relax, see a horizon and blackness for a moment… let these feelings of relaxation spread throughout your body. Let your relaxation deepen with each breath.

Nature is the home of women and men. In this guided imagery you will go deep into nature and experience the being ness of the presence of the sacred earth. In your mind's eye go to a place in nature that you love, a place that calls to you. It can be a mountain, a cave, a spring, a meadow, a river. Let the place come to you… it is your place in nature, the place in your life where the voices have come to you from mother earth. It may be place you went to as a child, a place where you went as a retreat to heal yourself, a place you go to now to refuel and balance. In your mind's eye be there, see it, feel it, smell it, hear it, touch it. Let all your senses fill with this special place.

Now go deeper. Listen to the sounds, let them come into your body. What do they tell you, what inner message is there for you in the voices of your place? See the visions of this beautiful place. Look deeper -- what do the visions show you, what do the voices say to you from the visions? What gift does this place give you? In your mind's eye go to each direction in this place, ask for a gift from nature, from the sacred earth, to you. You can ask for a gift to inform you about peace on earth or peace in your family. When you are at each direction, pause and let the gift come to you. See it, feel it, hear it, touch it, smell it. Then give an offering to this place in nature. Finally ask the place what it tells you about your life as a Caritas peacemaker… what lesson does this place give you?

When you are ready, return to the room where you are doing the exercise. First move your feet and then move your hands. Move them around and experience the feeling of the movement. Press your feet down onto the floor, feel the grounding, feel the pressure on the bottom of your feet, feel the solidity of the earth. Feel your backside on the chair; feel your weight pressing downwards. Now open your eyes. Look around you. Stand up and stretch, move your body, feel it move. You are back; you can carry the experience of the exercise outward to your life. You will feel stronger and be able to see deeper. You will be in a healing state. Each time you do the exercise you will be more relaxed and be able to go deeper and be more deeply healed.

CHAPTER TWELVE

CARITAS PROCESS 9. MEETING BASIC NEEDS: WAR IS CAUSED BY THIS NOT HAPPENING

For Caritas, basic needs means caring- for people's need for a healthy life, for nutrition, food, rest, comfort, and safety. To promote peace at individual level as well as community level is to care for people. Basic needs is dealing with physical, emotional, spiritual, well-being at the fundamental level.

POVERTY AND THE DIVINE FEMININE

Conquering poverty gives people control over their own lives and the lives of their children. Decreasing poverty is treating a basic need. Caritas peacemakers can teach people about how to be healthy in their environment; and in the specific countries where people live, feed and care for children, education is healing for peace. Caritas peacemakers can promote peace by promoting health literacy.

These things are basic diet, exercise, rest, social support, positive attitudes, and beliefs about health. The caritas peacemaker as teacher can create understanding about health and create a field of energy for peace. This book is to bring together caritas peacemakers so they can re -light the beacon of peace around the world.

Caritas peacemakers are manifestation of the divine feminine. The divine feminine meets needs. The divine feminine is the sacred energy in the world today. We call on caritas peacemakers world wide to shift the world's consciousness to peace, as the manifestation of the divine feminine on earth today. Foundations are shattered; today is a special time for women to step up and take their place and be heard as the voice of the feminine oracle of future.

We want to call forth more highly evolved human consciousness that connects human with nature and cosmos. In a moment, the past, present, and future become what we believe right now. We want to experience our lives with reverence and discover the radiance and beauty of the feminine. The divine feminine oracle says this, "It is time to honor the divine feminine as she who meets basic needs, to honor ourselves ,each other, and all living things. It is time." This requires transforming what you believe is important in the world, and allowing and inviting new possibilities.

In the world, words are used as weapons- you have an opponent- you must do battle - this requires winning, conquering, or defeating. It's a war against cancer, a war against terror, a war against drugs, a war against hunger. We have separated ourselves by ideas, we are separate -not connected. We separate, we do not live in balance or relationship. Meeting basic needs for peace is about balance and relationships. This shapes all our actions and thoughts, it is destructive. It has created the reality we live in. Through the divine feminine sacred, we need to create another world view that is life generating.

THE DIVINE FEMININE AND CARING AND PEACE

Remember ancient traditions- remember the past, remember enduring truths of wisdom. The feminine brings wisdom back – it is she who brings order from chaos. Sophia is a dramatic feminine energy who brings wisdom that permeates all things. In love we find joy, delight, and creation. Sophia defends the poor, leading us to wholeness; it is the only thing that makes us whole.

Basic needs is this: nursing practiced by women primarily with the mission of healing the sick, helping the poor, relieving suffering. The nursing solution is to minister to needs on a fundamental level – to attend birth, sickness, death, suffering, disease, to attend to basic needs. Nurses treat wounded soldiers-- all through history have given them food, water, cleanliness. This has been going on since the beginning of time. Now is no different. This book is calling to women and men to the divine feminine to meet the needs of our world for peace: the basic need for peace. We are the ones we are waiting for- if you don't do it, who will? My hand reaches out -touches your hand- come. My eyes look into your eyes. Basic needs- ice chips, water, , food, baths ,clean-up, pain relief.

Women protect the web of life, are its creators, give birth. They know the mysteries of the body are one. As the protectors of the soul of the living earth, they discover the roots of violence..

You would think that poverty and hunger cause war, but it is just the opposite. War causes poverty and hunger; the male patriarchal hierarchal culture wages war to make money and to keep the hierarchy of rich and poor. It creates hunger and maintains poverty by shifting resources to war from people. It is time for someone to change this. You are the one.

The relationship between basis needs and war has long been discussed. John Burton has been identified with the theory of basic human needs and war. The theory postulates the existence of universal needs that must be satisfied if people are to prevent or resolve destructive conflicts. Paul Sites defined eight essential needs whose satisfaction was required in order to produce "normal" (non-deviant, non-violent) individual behavior. According to Sites, these included the primary needs for consistency of response, stimulation, security, and recognition, and derivative needs for justice, meaning, rationality, and control. Abraham Maslow placed basic needs under five headings: physiological, safety, belongingness/love, esteem, and self-actualization.

Andrew Gavin Marshall has said, "We cannot afford to ignore the relationship between war, poverty and race. The poor are made to fight the poor; both are often disproportionately people of color. Yet war enriches the upper class, at least powerful sects of it in industry, the military, oil and banking. In a war economy, death is good for business, poverty is good for society, and power is good for politics. Western nations, particularly the United States, spend hundreds of billions of dollars a year to murder innocent people in far-away impoverished nations, while the people at home suffer the disparities of poverty, class, gender and racial divides. We are told we fight to 'spread freedom' and 'democracy' around the world; yet, our freedoms and democracy erode and vanish at home. You cannot spread what you do not have."

As George Orwell wrote: "The war is not meant to be won, it is meant to be continuous. Hierarchical society is only possible on the basis of poverty and ignorance. This new version is the past and no different past can ever have existed. In principle the war effort is always planned to keep society on the brink of starvation. The war is waged by the ruling group against its own subjects, and its object is not the victory over either Eurasia or East Asia, but to keep the very structure of society intact."

The chalice is the opposite of war, it is about woman as the receptacle, as the holding earth. Carrying the flow of life, giving birth, maintaining harmony of birth means maintaining peaceful existence -- what it means to be human.

In many ancient cultures

There must be a balance yin and yang for peace in the world. This is not a model of domination; it is a model of equality and partnership. The model of the future is not hierarchal; it is about energies in harmony.

OUTGROWING WAR

Matthew Fox speaks of humans now outgrowing war. "A civilization built on dualism and war within and between persons, one that puts its most creative minds and its best engineers to sadistic work building more and more destructive weapons, is no civilization at all. It needs a radical transformation from the heart outwards. It needs to outgrow and outlaw war just as in the last century it outlawed slavery. The human race has outgrown war, but it hardly knows it yet." He writes about war, the warrior and the feminine.

"Aggression is in all of us. Whether you're athlete or preacher, businessperson or taxi driver, aggression will emerge. It's easy to identify the negative ways it expresses itself: as war, as conquest (whether in business or sex), as passivity (aggression turned against oneself: "I can't do that..."), as selfish competition ("I can't win unless you lose") and more. But what are the healthy ways to engage it? How to turn aggression into nobility, to use Berry's term? To me, the key is understanding the distinction between a warrior and a soldier. A Vietnam veteran who volunteered to go to war at 17 described this eloquently: 'When I was in the army, I was a soldier. I was a puppet doing whatever anybody told me to do, even if it meant going against what my heart told me was right. I didn't know nothing about being a warrior until I hit the streets and marched alongside my brothers for something I really believed in. When I found something I believed in, a higher power found me.' He quit being a soldier and became a warrior when he followed his soul's orders, not his officer's; in his case, this meant protesting war and going to jail for it. The late Buddhist meditation master Chögyam Trungpa talks about the 'sad and tender heart of the warrior.' The warrior is in touch with his heart—the joy, the sadness, the expansiveness of it.

"However, not everyone understands this distinction. I believe the confusion of soldier and warrior feeds militarism and the reptilian brain. It's also an expression of homophobia, since I suspect heterosexism is behind much of the continued ignorance and fear of the real meaning of warriorhood. The warrior, unlike the soldier, is a lover. The warrior is so much in touch with his heart that he can give it to the world. The warrior loves not only his nearest kin and mate but also the world and God. The warrior relates to God as a lover.

"How different is this from right-wing depictions of God as judge and not lover? This view of God leads to the distortions of masculinity. The confusion of warrior and soldier feeds unhealthy relationships, with God, self and society. It feeds empire-building, and the builders of empire would like nothing more than to enlist young men who believe soldiering equals warriorhood. We can't afford this ignorance any longer. Nothing could be further from the truth."

CHAPTER THIRTEEN

CARITAS PROCESS 10. MIRACLES, PRAYERS AND OFFERINGS FOR PEACE

OUR OFFERING IS OURSELVES.

Open to the mystery... allow miracles to enter. This book is a prayer for peace. We need to go into our own inner spiritual and visionary journey, find our own place of peace within. Then we can come outwards from our heart and send peace to the world. Our heart is one with love and God. God is love, God is everywhere within every living thing. Our breath is God's breath. The guru is you. When you pray for peace, the energy of the whole world changes. When you pray for peace, your energy changes. Praying foe peace in community increases the power of the prayers. Prayers for peace lead to actions.

Our offering to world peace is ourselves, our offering is our life as we are living it. We offer our mind, our body, our voice, our spirit. We do this to raise ourselves to a higher frequency and energy and to become people of peace. As we gather more and more of us together, we recognize our allies. We recognize others and know who we are more deeply. The peace movement is growing like a sisterhood, a huge family. It will give energy to the earth like the ley lines of power in England. Places of prayer take on the energy of the prayers. The place itself becomes sacred and powerful. Churches, temples, mosques, ancient stone circles, mountains, caves and springs have become living prayers for peace.

THE PRAYER FOR PEACE

A prayer is a vision in our mind held and sent out to create reality. Its formulated with intent in a hope for the future and it asks something beyond us, a higher power, for help in manifesting this prayer on earth.

Our thoughts and prayers manifest into the reality of life as we know it. We pray that life will change. When we pray for starving children, our life may look the same but it helps them. . This consciousness grows around planet like web. Not like the world wide web through a computer system but through matrices which are transformational. In visionary space, as every prayer intersects another there is a point of light. As one crosses the path of another, there is intense energy. We may not speak, we may not recognize each other, but our prayers create a web of golden threads spun in spirit space. We will weave a web of peace around our planet… we can move global consciousness in prayers.

This is real, perfectly capable of happening. We want you to participate; everyone can do this. We will do this one person at a time. This begins with you. You may be first, last, in the middle. For every one of us, the first step is our first step. It is simple; we devote ourselves to a vision of world peace. We pray for peace in whatever way is comfortable.. You pray for peace alone, in groups, in a organized vigil, whenever you want to.

A PRAYER IS A DREAM SONG FOR PEACE.

There is a prayer song: "Let there be peace on earth, and let it begin with me." Ritual prayer and songs have always been a part of making peace happen. Energy healing and prayer have been shown to effect reality. Prayer makes plants grow and effects bacteria. Prayer effects healing and helps patients heal faster. In this crisis the first thing to do is vision and pray for peace.

THE METHOD

1. First: pray.

- Wake up to prayer.
- Have a prayer book or prayer journal.
- Write down your prayers.
- Write your concerns for family, friends, for yourself.
- Create an peace altar with sacred objects.
- Put your prayers on the altar.

- Bring in God, Jesus, The Blessed Mother, Allah, whoever you pray to.
- Pray to all the definitions of the God who receives our prayers.

We are creating peace in an act of faith. Writing your prayers down in the physical world is the first step.

2. Second: kindle faith

Light a candle in your world – it reminds us of our faith

3. Third: turn your prayers into right action

- Offering of our own life
- As we move out of prayerful meditation, we move into our life as offering.
- In prayer we can go out the door in action.
- All we need to do, is make our life what we do.
- Our life as an offering- maintains our integrity of prayer.
- We hold in our space the prayer, and God the receiver.
- We become in service to God.
- We become the answer to our prayer in the lives of others.
- By offering comfort, reassurance, gratitude, we recognize and pay attention.
- By listening we offer ourselves as the answer to our own prayer.
- We exhibit prayer by being in relationship to others.
- We move out of ourselves to answer our own prayer-- but we answer the prayer for others.

A FIRST STEP FOR PEACE IS TO MEDITATE THROUGH YOUR DAY.

Devote one hour a day to this goal. We do not need to even stop our lives to do this. We can be washing dishes, driving in a carpool, doing our jobs at the same time. Devote one hour a day in meditation to world peace even as we keep working. The momentum will get larger and larger… the vibrational energy of the earth will shift. We can shift consciousness worldwide. We can pray for world peace while we do other things. We are experts on doing more than one thing at once, we are good at this. Do this as part of your daily activities. If everyone did a meditation for peace for one hour a day, it would change their life decisions and change their life. Do what you do now. You do not need to do one more thing. Just do what you do with prayer and intention for peace.

Do what you do with integrity and a full heart. It feeds the world and feeds your soul. If you do not do what feeds your soul and if you do not receive abundance in what you do, you need to look at that. Click into the flow. What energy or force moves through you in what you do? It is like plugging into the right circuit; it comes through you and becomes accessible to the world. You become truly powerful, you become a transformer. The light of love and peace will flow through you.

Mary's question:

"I believe my thoughts and prayers manifest as reality. Anything I have ever asked for I have received. I believed this as a child. That is not to say it comes to you in the form or package or color or at the time you ask. That is the promise of this book; ask and you shall receive. We are given by God what we need to be given. We have been given dreams and the thoughts of the possibility of peace. We have been given free will to manifest peace. This is a challenge to insipient rage, despair, hurt and anger. It is a challenge to each of us not to act with destructive feelings. We feel these feelings but move to a place of grace. What do women do with their rage, pain, sorrow, grief, hunger, and unmet needs? They are there, they are real, they hold us… that is part of the life we are living. We live with these emotions, these are real, we all have the winds of pain and despair, disappointment and tears. Inside those storms we walk the path of peace even as we feel rage and hurt.

"I am very confused now. This war sometimes makes my world view crumble under the patriarchal vision of war that has dominated humanity for centuries. When the war started, I was discouraged and dismayed. I prayed for peace as hard as I could. It did not happen. I am sure women have felt this way for thousands of years. Jewish women felt this before the holocaust, Native American women felt this before the white man came. It is time for a change. What can we do to change? Will our prayer for peace by answered?"

A INVITATION TO PEOPLE OF POWER TO MAKE PEACE

Taking guidance from the *Global Interfaith Prayer Vigil*, we reach out to spiritual visionaries around the world and invite them to join in the planetary work for world peace.

We call to spiritual leaders and spiritual people in every faith and spiritual tradition— we call to priests, ministers, monks, nuns, roshis, rabbis, reverends, gurus, masters, sheiks, shamans, swamis, healers, lamas, rinpoches, etc.—and their followers. We invite them to their own traditions to find the most effective practices, prayers, meditation techniques, fasting, mantras, chants, visualizations, or ritual ceremonies for peace.

EXAMPLES OF SPECIFIC PRAYERS FOR PEACE

Prayers for peace from many different traditions were posted on the internet from various groups participating in the Global Interfaith Prayer Vigil, a vigil which took place from March to May 2003 to help stop the war in Iraq.

A Buddhist Prayer

A Prayer to Avert Nuclear War

by Chatral Rinpoche

Namo Guru Ratnatraya! To the Teacher and the Three Jewels I bow.
True leader of the golden age – Crown of the Sakyas!
Second Buddha, Prince of Oddiyana, Lake-Born Vajra,
Bodhisattvas – eight closest spiritual heirs
High Nobles, Avilokitesvara and Manjushri,
Vajrapani and the rest!
Twenty-one Taras, Host of Noble Elders,
Root and lineage lamas, deities,
Peaceful and wrathful gods!
Dakinis in your three homes!
(the earth, the heavens and the emanated worlds!)
You who through wisdom or karma have become Defenders of the
Doctrine!
Guardians of the Directions!
Seventy-five Glorious Protectors!
You who are clairvoyant, powerful, magical and mighty!
Behold and ponder the beings of this age of turmoil!
We are beings born at the sorry end of time;
An ocean of ill-effects overflow from our universally bad actions.
The forces of light flicker,
The forces of darkness, a demon army, inflames great and powerful
men.
And they rise in conflict, armed with nuclear weapons
That will disintegrate the earth.
The weapon of perverse and errant intentions
Has unleashed the hurricane.
Soon, in an instant, it will reduce the world
And all those in it to atoms of dust.
Through this ill-omened devils' tool
It is easy to see, to hear and to think about
Ignorant people caught in a net of confusion and doubt,
Are obstinate and still refuse to understand.
It terrifies us just to hear about or to remember
This unprecedented thing.
The world is filled with uncertainty,
But there is no means of stopping it, nor place of hope,

Other than you, undeceiving Three Jewels and Three Roots,
(Buddhas, Teaching and Spiritual Community, Lama, Deity and Dakini)
If we cry to you like children calling their mother and father,
If we implore you with this prayer,
Do not falter in your ancient vows!
Stretch out the lightning hand of compassion!
Protect and shelter us defenseless beings, and free us from fear!
When the mighty barbarians sit in council of war
- barbarians who rob the earth of pleasure and happiness
- barbarians who have wrong, rough, poisonous thoughts.
Bend their chiefs and lieutenants
To the side of peace and happiness!
Pacify on the spot, the armed struggle that blocks us!
Turn away and defeat the atomic weapons
Of the demons' messengers
And by that power, make long the life of the righteous,
And spread the theory and practice of the doctrine
To the four corners of this great world!
Eliminate root, branch and leaf – even the names
Of those dark forces, human and non-human,
Who hate others and the teaching!
Spread vast happiness and goodness
Over this fragile planet!
Elevate it truly with the four kinds of glory!
And as in the golden age, with all strife gone,
Let us be busy only with the dance of pleasure, the dance of joy1
We pray with pure thoughts –
By the compassion of that ocean the three supreme refuges
And the power of the Realm of Truth;
The complete sublime truth,
Achieve the goal of this, our prayer
Magically, just as we have hoped and dreamed!

Translated from the Tibetan by Richard Kohn and Lama Tsedrup Tharchin

The Great Invocation

From the point of Light within the Mind of God
Let light stream forth into the minds of men
Let Light descend on Earth
From the point of Love within the Hearth of God
Let love stream forth into the hearts of men
May Christ return on Earth
From the centre where the Will of God is known
Let purpose guide the little wills of men
The purpose which the Masters know and serve
From the centre which we call the race of men
Let the Plan of Love and Light work out
And may it seal the door where evil dwells
Let Light and Love and Power restore the Plan on Earth
Today and for all the Eternity. Amen.

This Invocation or Prayer does not belong to any person or group but to all Humanity. The beauty and the strength of this Invocation lies in its simplicity, and in its expression of certain central truths which all men, innately and normally, accept: the truth of the existence of a basic Intelligence to Whom we vaguely give the name of God; the truth that behind all outer seeming, the motivating power of the universe is Love; the truth that a great Individuality came to earth, called by Christians, the Christ, and embodied that love so that we could understand; the truth that both love and intelligence are effects of what is called the Will of God; and finally the self-evident truth that only through humanity itself can the Divine Plan work out.

Alice A. Bailey

How to make a miracle

A miracle is difficult to define. It's usually thought of as an unexpected happening, unlikely or impossible or against the odds. It is sometimes attributed to divine intervention of God, Goddess or greater power. Often it is attributed to someone like a saint or angel or miracle worker. A miracle is often thought of as a happening that violates the laws of nature or is unexplainable by them. For many people, miracles are also non-religious, statistically unlikely or especially wonderful happenings such as survival of a terminal illness, or escaping a life threatening situation.

GUIDED IMAGERY : BRINGING IN THE LIGHT

You can experience the healing power of light right now. Bringing in the light is a practice that concentrates light and love in your life. It brings incredible energy to you for healing; it surrounds you with a dome of light that comes up from the earth and down from the sky at once. When you bring in the light, you are also bringing in healing vision… you are calling your spirit to open his or her eyes and see. As you do the exercise, look for the God's or Goddess's face above you. When you make a dome of light, He or She appears in the center and blesses you. Bringing in the light heals you, others, and your surroundings.

When you bring in the light, you are embraced by the love of the universe. You are embraced by the earth and healing forces of the earth. Bringing in the light is done with conscious intent. Close your eyes and perform the exercise. When you are illuminated you can hear the voice of your spirit clearly and your intuition is sharp.

Find a place that you love or that is sacred for you. It can be the top of the mountain or any other place that calls you. You can do this exercise alone or with another person. If you bring in the light with a partner, stand apart, look at each other, look deep into their eyes, and do it together.

First, pause, give thanks for your beauty and for being a Caritas peacemaker. Now close your eyes. Put your arms at your side and relax. Open your eyes. Now slowly, very slowly, raise your arms upwards until they almost touch over your head. Now touch your hands together at the top. It is as if you are pointing upwards. As you raise your arms, see the light from the earth getting brighter and brighter. It is as if you are creating a sacred dome of light around you. The dome of light rises and rises and when your arms are together at the top it is complete. Now slowly bring your hands apart and down to each side. This brings the light down over you and the earth and holds it there.

Now bring your arms to the front of your body and make a cup with your hands. This will bring the love and light from above into your heart more deeply. Stand in the light and feel its beauty and brightness. This is the sacred light on earth. When you can see His or Her face in the center of the light, you are receiving a great gift.

When you see Him or Her bring in the light, you see Him or Her. You see Him or Her from before, from previous life times, from before time, from everywhere at once. He and She dissolve and come back together in each stellar moment. It is beautiful beyond belief. When you see Him or Her bring in the light you are taken deep into timelessness and spacelessnes, into His or Her heart forever. You can feel the energy, see more deeply than you ever have, go through the veil and see His or Her face.

Section Three

EMBODYING PEACE AS ACTION

CHAPTER FOURTEEN

YOUR INNER VOICE OF WISDOM FOR PEACE

There is a place within you that holds the wisdom of the earth. It is a place within your center that you can draw from as you walk your path for peace. This place is an inner embodied wisdom, a part of you connected to the wholeness of the universe. It's a place within you that is in balance and harmony and holds your natural flow of serenity and peace. There are many ways to access this inner voice of wisdom. Praying is a way to speak to God from the place of wisdom, or we can speak from it to ourselves. This is a place where we may access spiritual guidance and benefit from a spiritual presence. It may be accessed by feeling its energy or heard through songs or inner voices. It can be as subtle as a voice on the wind, or sound like you are amongst the angels. Or it can feel like a spirit guide or the voice of an ancestor. The experience of the inner voice of wisdom has no boundaries in how its form manifests. When we connect with the voices within- we are connecting to the living wisdom that surrounds us.

Our task is to make this experience within your life clearer and more apparent and to help you to develop a relationship with this place that makes it clearer in your life. You may experience the inner voice of wisdom as you move more gently through your own life. Your inner wisdom keeper will inform you as a Caritas peacemaker. The inner wisdom keeper has been waiting to communicate with you- its own wisdom becomes accessible to you like a familiar memory. This aspect of yourself embodies the consciousness of the living earth.

Some people hear inner voices that inform their lives. It feels like an idea or thought, but the cadence of language and way it feels is unusual. You know it is right. It is like a convincing dream. Inner voices often appear when a person is depressed and confused. In the sadness and lack of decision about your life, you can hear an inner voice. Validate its advice with small actions and see how it works out. The inner voice is often called a spirit guide or inner guide. Other people hear the trees speak, the wind, the waters speak. Often children hear voices in nature singing to them.

Think of a decision you needed to make in your life. It can be as simple as where you wanted to camp or as complex as taking a job or continuing with a relationship. Find a memory in your past where you had a clear intuition or sudden clear knowledge of what to do. Suddenly, making a clear choice was easy; you knew your decision was correct. For example, when you found the campsite or place to stop you knew the place was right, this felt right. If you look deeper into the memory you may realize that you had a moment of hearing the mountain tell you, "this is the place", or you had a clear inner voice say, "this is it." We have these moments all the time. They are as ordinary and breathing, yet as wonderful as the sun coming up. What is the voice that tells you this is right? You ask yourself, is she the woman for me? An answer comes to you from within, "Yes, I love her, yes this is the woman I want to spend my life with." The inner voice that helps you make these decisions can be thought of as your wisdom voice. It is a special part of you that knows what your heart feels, knows what the earth wants, knows God. It is the voice that you hear when you meditate or pray. It happens to all of us. It is part of being human.

Each of us has many of these inner voices; we all have an inner voice of wisdom for peace. This voice is the voice that spoke to the Caritas peacemaker, the voice that speaks to all Caritas peacemakers throughout time.

A GUIDED IMAGERY FOR LISTENING TO THE VOICE OF THE CARITAS PEACEMAKER WITHIN

This guided imagery will help you meet your Caritas peacemaker within. The voice of the Caritas peacemaker within comes from deep within her consciousness, and is one of our deepest memories.

Close your eyes. Take a couple of deep breaths, letting your abdomen rise and fall. Go into your imagery space as you have many times before. Now put yourself on a path. Feel your feet touch the earth, smell the fresh air, feel the warm breeze on your face. Walk down the path. It goes downhill slightly. The ground is hard and has small stones in the soil. It is solid and secure. Feel the ground and the grass that is on each side of the path. Now the path crosses a wooden bridge across a rushing stream. The bridge has stout railings. You can hear your feet echo on the bridge like a drumbeat as you walk across. Perhaps you need to drop something in the water that you want to get rid of. Do that now.

After the stream, the path now goes upwards slightly and comes over a rise. Below you is a large meadow. In the center of the meadow is a grassy circle. Sit in the circle and wait. With you in the circle are your friends and teachers, people who support you in this work. Drift and dream. See the circle become magical, and feel yourself awakening to magic.

Now ask for your Caritas peacemaker within to come to you. Ask for the Caritas peacemaker to come to you to tell you what you need to do to make world peace. Invite the Caritas peacemaker within to come up from your memories or come from afar. In inner space, look around- you can see behind you, all around you in inner space. Let the figure appear and come up to you. It can come from a distance or appear right next to you. It may appear suddenly or slowly. Let the figure come towards you. It may even begin to speak to you. It will speak in an inner voice that sounds to you like a thought- but feels like it is not yours alone. You can ask your Caritas peacemaker within a question, you can ask why she has come to you and what she will help you do. Inner wisdom figures may not always speak in words; they may speak in riddles or in feelings. You can speak to them and tell them what you want. Tell your Caritas peacemaker within you will visit him, speak to him and be with them.

You can stay in the meadow as long as you wish. Your Caritas peacemaker within is part of the earth. It has tendrils that reach deep into the earth, the sky, and you, connecting them all together. If you feel comfortable, let the Caritas peacemaker touch you… even come into your body. You can merge with your Caritas peacemaker and see out of his or her eyes.

When you are ready to leave, say good by to your Caritas peacemaker within, stand up and leave the meadow. The path goes out of the far side of the circle and you can walk down the path further. It leads to the edge of an ancient forest of old growth trees. Stand at the edge of the forest by a great ancient tree. Find a tree that beckons you. Now put your hand on the tree… touch its rough back. Feel its warmth, its life. Now imagine that when you put your hand on the tree, you move deep into the spiral of your own being. You spiral deep inside yourself, into your heart, and inside your body. Your heart opens with wings. A spirit eye opens within you and sees this experience. It witnesses you becoming the Caritas peacemaker .

Walk back to the meadow, then to the bridge, then to where you are now. Bring your Caritas peacemaker within. Bring the connectedness with you. Now move your feet. Look around you. You are now on *The Path to a Peaceful Life*. You can see and hear ideas for peace. You can hear a wisdom voice telling you how to make peace on earth.

The Caritas peacemaker within is a wisdom keeper of the earth's energy and magic. When we see out of the eyes of the Caritas peacemaker, we hear the wisdom that resonates within ancient sages about the earth's energy. We hear how to be in balance and harmony with the earth. We hear how to be one with the earth. That is the message they have for us.

HOW TO HEAR YOUR INNER CARITAS PEACEMAKER SPEAK

Once we have a Caritas peacemaker within, we need to listen to her and let her speak. The Caritas peacemakers for Peaces come as guardians, to help us make peace. We need to hear their voices to benefit from their presence fully. Their power comes to us by their presence. We see them in visions and they accompany us on our peacemaking journeys. They give us the power of ancient wisdom and the healing way of the Caritas peacemaker. The Caritas peacemaker speaks from her heart to your heart. You hear it in your mind, body, and being. How do you hear the voice of the Caritas peacemaker within? Within the mystical silence, it reverberates in your head. It is the same way you hear music in your mind. It *reverberates*.

HOW TO HEAR THE VOICES OF INNER WISDOM

When a voice of inner wisdom speaks to you, you will feel it as thoughts that are clearer, more focused, and sound slightly different than the ordinary. They may have a new cadence of words, an accent, a new way of speaking. It is subtle. Ask for the Caritas peacemaker within or inner voice of wisdom to speak to you, then listen and pay attention to the thoughts you are having. If your mind wanders, as is natural, bring it back.

Your goal is to be able to receive a clear coherent message from your voice of wisdom with a teaching and a theme that you can remember and use in your life. It takes practice, but it will happen. As you listen to the voices of your Caritas peacemakers for Peace within more and more, you will be able to understand them better as they call to you in the physical world. The messages from your Caritas peacemakers for Peace come back to you whenever you remember their face or voice. The inner voice and feeling is a pointer to the message.

YOU NEED TO QUIET DOWN TO HEAR THE INNER VOICES OF WISDOM

To hear inner voices it is essential that you quiet down. You need to create a mystical silence away from the material world where you call them and invite them to come. Quiet down, invite wisdom voices and they will come. Take a walk, paddle on a river, hike in the mountains. Go to a park. Listen with your inner ear, not to sounds… see in your inner eye, not sights, and they will come to you. There is a pause, a moment of rest, then they will start telling you the story. It will sound like your own thoughts but different-- clearer, straight-forward, like listening to a voice with its own character. It is the inner voice of the living earth speaking as your own inner voice.

Listen to the stories when they come to you. They can be long. They are clearest as poetry, as a story, as a vision. They will tell you what you are to do in your life. Ask a question. Listen to your wisdom voice for an answer. You will receive messages and teachings, but they are not always direct. They have been riddles since the beginning of time. In a riddle, there is room for you to enter, for your own voice to fill in and make it relate to your life. Then the communion of your wisdom voice and you happens, and it is the world being created. The wisdom voice will tell you what you need to know to grow, and what you need to do to make peace in this lifetime. Because it is from a wisdom voice, it will always be about making the world sacred, saving the animals and the earth, making peace, healing and balance. That is the voice you are tapping into. Be specific about which voice you want to hear. That is the one who will answer. If you want a voice of peace, of balance, that is who you will get. Voices of pure greed are not here. Wisdom voices speak only in balance.

CREATE YOUR OWN STORIES FROM THE WISDOM VOICES.

You will hear the wisdom voice and then create your own stories with your capacity for intuitive wisdom and imagination. Your thoughts will come to you like a creative idea, like a voice, a vision, a thought. If it is a vision, you will see it by simply picturing it in your mind. Open yourself to these images. Use your imaginary eye.

HOW TO USE THE WISDOM VOICES AS INTUITION:

They speak to you in signs – a person telling you something, a website, a new friend, a march, a vision. The language of inner voices can be silence. People who have pets know this; their pets talk to them as knowledge, as inner thoughts, as emotions. The inner voices are a doorway to deep intuitive realizations. The message comes to you as an intuitive thought.

Inner wisdom sometimes communicates to you without words, below words. It is a gut feeling, a feeling in your heart of being one with something, of being moved and touched, of being taken care of and loved. When you put it into words it says, "I love you, thank you for listening to me, I want to be heard, I want you to help make peace for yourself, others, and the earth." It reverberates within for peace.

One of the ways to get in touch with this part of yourself is to get in touch with the voice within you that emerges from your heart. Center, and take deep breaths. Find the place inside you with a deeper vibrational level. It is between the heart and the belly. There is a voice from the very center of your beingness. The voice is vibration at a spiritual level that interfaces with a greater power. Go inside to this clear place which transcends personality- go to the place with the quality of timelessness. Go to your place within which transcends your lifetime, go deep within and embrace that part of you. It has a quality of palpable fullness, a depth. You can hear the voice emerge from within yourself. It's the voice of your own with clarity and inner wisdom, it is larger than your life. It transcends your personality, it transcends your gender, it transcends your lifetime. It is almost like it's the accumulation of all the lifetimes that have walked before you. Suddenly, with the emergence of the inner voice, you have access to collective and universal wisdoms. You have access to part of yourself that is interrelated and interconnected to the vibration quality of all of life.

When I speak with this voice, I am deeply connected to all living things. It is as if the inner voice itself is an oracle. It heeds an inner warning to situations and also has an openness to newness and mystery. It can see though chaos with a perspective that embraces the spaciousness of thoughts. It comes from the same place that you hold in meditation, the place of spaciousness. It comes from the place where the inner voice and inner witness merge. When you cultivate the inner voice of wisdom, it takes you to a place of vast spaciousness like the universe itself. It is literally within the experience of the expansiveness of consciousness; it is literally within the vibration quality of alertness and sensitivity. It is the vibrational quality of life. Here there is no right or wrong, no emotions. It is on a primal level; it expands and becomes large enough to embrace the body, mind, thoughts, feelings. It holds your whole condition of humanness. The inner voice of wisdom comes from a place from within that is larger than you. This place has a feeling of peace.

The inner wisdom voice is she or he who talks in ritual. Whoever that person is who comes out, is surprising and beyond your mind and intelligence. When you lead a ritual and speak, a beautiful voice emerges from deep within that holds more knowledge than you have. What is the place within you, that you go to, that speaks in brilliance and illumination? It needs to be large enough to hold your life, large enough to hold the world of dissent. To be a Caritas peacemaker, you have to have a world view large enough to hold the world of conflicting points of view. To hold people who think they are right and think you are wrong. As a Caritas peacemaker you have to be large enough to hold warring aspects of yourself within you. You have to be able to step over your insecurities and choose a path of clarity and direction. You have to be able to step over obstacles within yourself to move forward with conviction and expansiveness.

CHAPTER FIFTEEN

FEMININE ENERGY FOR PEACE

PEACE IS A WOMAN'S JOB

Many of us are having the slow realization that the solution to this world crisis is a woman's job. Women are sensitive to emotion and energy. They have a natural nurturing instinct which includes appreciation for this earth and its animals. They know about children, the weak, the oppressed, the innocent. Women do not cause war or go to war, women have sons who are taken.

The world is now populated with increasing numbers of women that see. Like seers, priestesses of old, witches, oracles, healers, they know the future and the present; they know about energy and healing. It has been a long time coming. It is a reaction to the patriarchal system that has oppressed them for millennia.

Now women need to help make peace. They need to become the spiritual leaders again, as they were for thousands of years. We speak to all women: You are the earth. Your body needs to be healed. Do this with energy and love. It is energetic you will change the structure of the earth. You have been through it all; you have done the necessary suffering and developed skills to make you a Caritas peacemaker. In your mothering, you know how to care for everything.

Now is the new time of turning up the volume. Do work each week with energetic connections. What is actually happening is not what it looks like is going on. It is war but it's also an opening for peace. It is a losing of everything and then a prayer to move energy. Each person who prays changes the whole world. Each person who prays for peace creates peace. The earth is calling out for healing. Words have been spoken that are like a toxic poison… the world prays, speaks, and calls for peace and healing.

A WAKE UP CALL FOR CARITAS PEACEMAKERS TO EMERGE

This world crisis is the wake up call for the woman healer to emerge. The terrorist attack of 9/11 was highly visible; the war in Iraq is highly visible. We saw it… all the women on the planet see it. Now is the time for the woman to save the earth and clean up the mess we are in. As she stands beside her husband in this crisis, we go to war. Look into your own heart. Do you want to send your young son to die? Do you want to take him and us to where all you see is your death? The goddess gave her only son to die for the world, it's been done already. You don't have to do it over and over again. Her son said, "Forgive them father, for they know not what they do." And they were forgiven. It's over, it's time for a new way of being; the old way of solving problems is over.

We know Her son did not die for nothing, he died for us. We gave our son; we gave our child for the earth. We know the sacrifice has been great. We talk about all children sacrificed for generations, from the crusades to Iraq, from the Middle East to Yugoslavia. Who is going to stop it? What's the next terrorist attack going to be-- chemical, biological, nuclear? What will the next war be? We will not participate. We know in our hearts as women we will stand apart from men who want war again. We will negotiate with other women in the world. We are CEO's, anchor women, movie stars, doctors. We are everywhere now-- lawyers, accountants, business women-- we are powerful women. This is the most import thing we can do.

We are an idealistic generation of free, educated, powerful women. We will change the world… we will change human consciousness. We will move toward new creative ways of peace through communication; we will make change in balance with the earth and the animals. The era of patriarchal power needs to end right now, before we destroy our planet. Do you doubt this? Look at the mess men have made. It is like a much bigger version of them leaving the kitchen after dinner and letting us clean it all up. The rivers are polluted, the air polluted, our dominant value is making money, mothering is not valued. We consume resources as if they are things… species are dying, old growth forests dying… what's next? He takes our children to war for what reason: revenge, hatred, that the big giant has awakened to stamp on children in faraway lands? We will not allow that; the children we are about to bomb are starving;

women can see they are just like our children. The truth is we can do something about it using our personal power. Women can act to do something in the world. For us to stand there and expect men to be different than they are has never worked. Look at your life. We need to be who we are. We do not need them to change… we can love them, let them be fathers, lovers, but not in control of war and peace anymore.

WOMEN NEED TO SPEAK OUT…

Women need to speak out loud with a passionate voice. We need to be strong. We are healers…we deal with children, we take care of old people when they die, we feed the world by feeding one person at a time in our family. We feed children so we feed the world- it is not a metaphor, it is completely real. Hatred is not acceptable any more; we see the eyes of the enemy and we know they are just like us. They have families, lovers, just like us; they have imperfections just like our imperfections. We are past the point of thinking we are perfect; we know we are imperfect, we are not trying to create a perfect world, just to create Caritas peacemakers for Peace.

For thousands of years it has been a patriarchal world, a world where one person dominates others. In the last years, woman's spirit has empowered itself. It started with books in the sixties like Woman's Room, then feminist politics, moon groups, Wicca, meditation, "Our Bodies Ourselves"… all played a role. Now after years of consciousness work and remembering, we are powerful… our power is emerging for peace. We are more powerful in diversity as women; we are Jewish, Christian, Buddhist, Hindu, Islam… we are awakened women in a global world. We need to take care of ourselves, and that means everyone.

We have seen the earth from the moon. There were no countries, no boundaries, no maps… the lines were not there. There was no separation. From the nighttime sky we saw the separation was only in the man's imagination. We are different; it is truly an illusion, we can see that now. There are no races; the DNA is exactly the same except for skin color. The only profound difference between people is between man and woman.

The power now is still with the male; he is and has been a warlike creature. He has done good things, invented things, created weapons that are awesome. It is time for him to rest and for us to move forward in a nurturing peaceful way. The world needs feminine healing right now. It is the moment we have been waiting for. It is now the time to stand up and speak and do action. If there ever was a time, it is now. We are on the brink of our own destruction. Don't hesitate for a second to act. Know you can and you will and it will make a difference.

TOWARDS A FEMININE WAY OF LOOKING AT THE EARTH

Are you willing to use your personal power to bring peace to the world?

This chapter is about a new way of looking at the world in peace. It is about a feminine way of looking at the earth, but it is not about feminism. It is a chapter about feminine power, sexuality, mothering. The female says, "I do not want more killing on earth. I am outraged by destruction; it is the destruction of our lives. Women, old men, children are being destroyed again and again and for what? For whom? This is a chapter about a nurturing, non patriarchal way of looking at the earth and peace. Although the chapter is about the feminine as the Caritas peacemaker it includes nurturing men who look at the world without seeing power, destruction, war, revenge and materialism.

The world is a mess. Men did it. It is time we stand up as women and nurturing awakened men. The world is on a threshold of great change. Women raise children, are in public office, are leaders in business, healthcare and politics. This is the time for women to unite for world peace. Many of us are tired of the patriarchal old world ways. Men also raise children; they are gardeners, healers, support and love women and children. It is time for non patriarchal men to unite for world peace.

MARRYING THE FEMININE AND MASCULINE

It may seem we swing the other way when we honor the feminine. Honoring the feminine is not at the expense of ignoring the masculine. The masculine is at the foundation of human civilization-equal to the feminine. The problem has been the suppression of the feminine, which allows the masculine to be larger than it should be. The masculine has been allowed to be perverse and unchecked. The masculine thrust of bombs and building needs to be counterbalanced with nurturing and caring. We must not underestimate the power of the voice of the feminine to say, "No, stop, this is not right action."

As opposed to the feminine alone or the masculine alone- we suggest feminine and masculine merge in love. When a man loves the feminine, when a woman loves the masculine, they both give and receive equally. This creates the balance that results in life and the life force for propagation.

The presence of feminine and masculine together is the truth of evolution; the force of life is to marry the two. God is both at once, God is feminine and masculine as one. Love emerges in union and communion with our feminine and masculine sides. This spiritual union between the two becomes one in each one of us. Our heartbeat literally comes from the coming together of the spiritual energy of the feminine and masculine. As we love, we merge the spirits of feminine and masculine lovers and are merged as humans. We become part of the merging of this love, and the love emerges in every aspect of our lives. Nature is the feminine and masculine giving birth to life. It is the real life force. And in becoming the lover or the beloved, we manifest the spiritual love emerging in the world right now, the communion of God's love in perfect communion with feminine and masculine.

As we live our lives and enact this love, we become illuminated. In the birth of this sacred union, we manifest God's love on earth and the earth's love for itself.

The path for peace is a spiritual practice of merging feminine and masculine with love and knowing how to create the balance in each situation. To do this is simple… all we need to do is honor what's been ignored, invalidated, invisible- the feminine love. The feminine voice and its values need to be honored to swing the pendulum back and create balance again. The practical advice is to honor and heed the feminine voice until balance is achieved.

In a conflict situation, see out of Her eyes… see out of Her and His eyes, as one. Be two as one, be one as two. Be in perfect love, being seen by Her in beauty. When two see, they merge and see as Him and Her. She enters, He enters. The two can be you and spirit, the two can be two people, lovers, patient and healer. Bring in pure love and She comes and heals, He comes and heals. The Goddess and God energy as one make peace. The feminine and masculine energy as one balance and heal the patriarchal zenith that has resulted in war. For peace there are no rules, no dogmatic ways. Making peace from war is like Nelson Mandela in prison, making beauty out of horror. Don't get attached, don't hold dogma. Do not recreate another way to suppress creativity; be open and creative enough to think about things that are out there without boxes.

THE LEGEND OF THE MERGING OF FEMALE AND MALE FOR PEACE

In an ancient legend, she saw him and fell in love. He saw her and fell in love. She said, "Do you want me to be your teacher for peace in the world or do you want to possess   me as a wife? The peace maker is who you have always been, I will take you there." She showed him peace, she taught him to listen to her voice, see out of her eyes. He saw her in the sunrise, the shadows, the moonrise. She came and went in spirit space, over him, making love. He was entranced totally. He saw the sun as her, he saw the light as her, he learned and then

ne man seeing her, and she awakens and peace is born."
in everything; then he worshipped her. His work became,
lis_ to her, making Her voice available on earth to make peace.
He made her speak, enabled her as she who makes peace to be heard.
He loved her beyond perfectly in every moment so she was seen, and
she awakened and peace was born on earth through the merging of
woman and man as one.

WOMEN ARE ACTUALLY INDISPENSABLE FOR PEACE

Swanee Hunt and Christina Posa of Women Waging Peace have said:

"International organizations are slowly recognizing the indispensable role that women play in preventing war and sustaining peace.
On October 31, 2000, the United Nations Security Council issued
Resolution 1325 urging the secretary-general to expand the role of
women in U.N. field-based operations, especially among military
observers, civilian police, human rights workers, and humanitarian
personnel.

"Approximately 80% of today's civilian casualties are women (Oxfam)
and 80% of all refugees and internally displaced people worldwide are women and children (United Nations High Commissioner
for Refugees). Civilian victims, mostly women and children often
outnumber casualties among combatants…women often become
carriers for injured combatants and find themselves unexpectedly
cast as the sole parent, manager of the household and caretakers
of elderly relatives. Parties to the conflict often rape women with
impunity, sometimes using systematic rape as a tactic of terrorism. The impact of violence against women and violations of their
human rights in such situations is experienced by women of all
ages, who suffer displacement, loss of home and property. (Beijing
Platform for Action - 1995).

"However, women are not simply passive victims. From Northern
Ireland to Burundi, from the Middle East to Colombia, women are

working towards constructing new visions of peace and security, which place human concerns at their center. In all their varied roles; as community leaders, social organizers, farmers, teachers, welfare workers etc. and despite overwhelming challenges against them women play a significant role in peace building and reconciliation processes within their communities."

"Allowing men who plan wars to plan peace is a bad habit. But international negotiators and policymakers can break that habit by including peace promoters, not just warriors, at the negotiating table. More often than not, those peace promoters are women. Certainly, some extraordinary men have changed the course of history with their peacemaking; likewise, a few belligerent women have made it to the top of the political ladder or, at the grass-roots level, have taken the roles of suicide bombers or soldiers. Exceptions aside, however, women are often the most powerful voices for moderation in times of conflict. While most men come to the negotiating table directly from the war room and battlefield, women usually arrive straight out of civil activism and—take a deep breath—family care." (Foreign Policy, issue 124, May-June 2001.)

Women waging peace at Harvard University has sponsored a research conference on women and peace. The conference reviewed research by Joshua Goldstein, Professor of International Relations at American University, and Richard Wrangham, Professor of Anthropology at Harvard University. These researchers explored the differences between men and women's proclivity to violence and peace from anthropological and biological points of view. They discussed the question of why men have the demonstrated tendency to be more aggressive. Wrangham presented his research conducted on primates, specifically Chimpanzees and Bonobos, two comparable species that both have close similarities to the genetic make-up of humans. He suggested a biological link to explain aggressive behavior in Chimpanzees and peaceful behaviors in Bonobos. Researchers also argue that many aggressive tendencies in men are the result of gender norms created by culture. Goldstein points out that societies tend to equate masculinity with warrior-like qualities. They thus capitalize on biological tendencies and train men to become more violent.

THE LYSISTRATA PROJECT.

Aristophanes, the Greek playwright, wrote Lysistrata in 413 B.C. Lysistrata ("releaser of war") called a gathering of the women of Athens and of Sparta, (with which Athens had been at war). She proposed that the women should refuse to have sex with their husbands and lovers until the men made peace. Women have taken this idea from Lysistrata and used it in creative ways for peace. The play has been performed in thousands of theatres. Letters to leaders have suggested that women withhold sex, food, childcare, all the things they do to take care of men, for peace, until the war is over.

Currently there are several groundbreaking organizations of women for peace. Women Waging Peace, Women of Vision and Action, (Wova) , Lysistrata, Gather the Women, and Women Building Peace all are working to gather women for peace.

WOMEN'S PEACE WEB LINKS

www.Peacesummit.org

www.wova.org

www.gatherthewomen.org

www.rootsofpeace.org

Swanee Hunt and Christina Posa Woman have said, "Women are often the most powerful voices for moderation in times of conflict. While most men come to the negotiating table directly from the war room and battlefield, women usually arrive straight out of civil activism and—take a deep breath—family care.

Today, the goal is not simply the absence of war, but the creation of sustainable peace by fostering fundamental societal changes.

The idea of women as Caritas peacemakers is supported by social science research which finds women as generally more collaborative than men and thus more inclined toward consensus and compromise."

CHAPTER SIXTEEN

RESOURCES FOR PEACE

Many people have written about philosophies and strategies for peaceful action. These statements are useful resources for peace.

CHRISTIANE NORTHRUP'S ADVICE FOR PEACE

Christiane Northrup, M.D, the well known physician and author, says that the fear and anxiety resulting from war is a large health problem. Realizing that emotions such as fear and anger impede the healing process and produce pain, fear, and anxiety, she recommends specific things each of us can do right now to help prevent war and create peace and health in our bodies, minds, and spirits. No one can be healthy with war around us. If the bombs don't kill us the stress and fear will.

Northrup recommends paying attention to your inner guidance. She says that each person has access to guidance from within that leads them in the right direction if they pay attention. She says, "Each of us has the power, through our thoughts and emotions, to influence the energy of the planet in a way that helps prevent further conflict and also creates peace."

Northrup recommends these steps to create peace and be healthy:

1. She reminds us that thoughts have power and manifest in reality. The consciousness you hold creates the kind of life you live. She says, "It's impossible to create peace and harmony if you're pushing up against a war. It's impossible to create peace and harmony if you're condemning George Bush, Dick Cheney, Colin Powell, Barack Obama. Create peace with peaceful thoughts of action.

2. To create peace, you need to be peaceful. The way to stop war is to start from within. She calls this, "personal disarmament". The way to stay peaceful is to concentrate on what brings you peace and to resist your own negative emotions. Change your thoughts and emotions from those of anger, hatred, and fear to those of compassion and peace. You can do this.

She suggests that you take 30 seconds several times a day to create a "virtual reality of what peace would look and feel like". She advises that you imagine in your minds eye a future where all is well. Using guided imagery, imagine a world where we can live as one and understand and accept other's cultures. When thinking about any enemy, imagine women and children and love. Send your energy and compassion to them as if they were your family.

3. Imagine all the angels and spirit beings protecting and uplifting us. Imagine them working in compassion, not hate. Imagine whatever higher power you believe in helping and blessing us with peace.

4. Northrup advises that you avoid watching TV news or reading newspapers. News is meant to raise fear and adrenaline so you will buy the products of the advertisers and buy newspapers. It creates fear. If you watch the news, choose stories that inform or uplift.

5. Last, she suggests that you tune into your heart, listen to your Inner Wisdom, and God. Then, you " become a beacon of light and peace. You become an uplifter and a Caritas peacemaker."

The Universal Declaration On Nonviolence: The Incompatibility of Religion and War

Religious leaders all over the earth have joined in collective vision to stop war and to create a new world of peace. This is new and exciting. The document below is a manifesto for peace by some of the religious leader of the world.

"This document is an attempt to set forth a vision of non-violence within the context of an emerging global civilization in which all forms of violence, especially war, are totally unacceptable as means to settle disputes between and among nations, groups, and persons. This new vision of civilization is global in scope, universal in culture, and based on love and compassion, the highest moral/spiritual principles of the various historical religions. Its universal nature acknowledges the essential fact of modern life: the interdependence of nations, economies, cultures, and religious traditions.

"As members of religious groups throughout the world, we are increasingly aware of our responsibility to promote peace in our age and in the ages to come. Nevertheless, we recognize that in the history of the human family, people of various religions, acting officially in the name of their respective traditions, have either initiated or collaborated in organized and systematic violence or war. These actions have at times been directed against other religious traditions, groups, and nations, as well as within particular religious traditions. This pattern of behavior is totally inappropriate for spiritual persons and communities. Therefore, as members of world religions, we declare before the human family, that:

"Religion can no longer be an accomplice to war, to terrorism or to any other forms of violence, organized or spontaneous, against any member of the human family. Because this family is one, global, and interrelated, our actions must be consistent with this identity. We recognize the right and duty of governments to defend the security of their people and to relieve those afflicted by exploitation and persecution. Nevertheless, we declare that religion must not permit itself to be used by any state, group or organization for the purpose of supporting aggression for nationalistic gain. We have an obligation to promote a new vision of society, one in which war has no place in resolving disputes between and among states, organizations, and religions.

"In making this declaration, we the signatories commit ourselves to this new vision. We call upon all the members of our respective traditions to embrace this vision. We urge our members and all peoples to use every moral means to dissuade their governments from promoting war or terrorism. We strongly encourage the United Nations organization to employ all available resources toward the development of peaceful methods of resolving conflicts among nations.

"Our declaration is meant to promote such a new global society, one in which nonviolence is preeminent as a value in all human relations. We offer this vision of peace, mindful of the words of Pope Paul VI to the United Nations in October 1965: "No more war: war never again!"

SIGNATORIES:

Thomas Keating, Johanna Becker, Wayne Teasdale, Dom Bede Griffiths, Raimundo Panikkar, Katherine Howard, Pascaline Coff, Theophane Boyd, Ruth Fox, Timothy Kelley, and other members of the North American Board for East-West Dialogue; and His Holiness the Dalai Lama

Promulgated and signed on April 2, 1991, at Santa Fe, NM, USA

THE NOT IN OUR NAME PLEDGE

Not in our Name is a leading organization for peace. It has sponsored and led peace marches and had been a voice for peace since the start of the Iraq crises. It has inspired songs by great songwriters/peace activists like John McCutcheon, Si Kahn and Pete Seeger. Here is their pledge from their website.

"THE PLEDGE OF RESISTANCE

We believe that as people living
in the United States it is our
responsibility to resist the injustices
done by our government,
in our names

Not in our name
will you wage endless war
there can be no more deaths
no more transfusions

of blood for oil

Not in our name
will you invade countries
bomb civilians, kill more children
letting history take its course
over the graves of the nameless

Not in our name
will you erode the very freedoms
you have claimed to fight for

Not by our hands
will we supply weapons and funding
for the annihilation of families
on foreign soil

Not by our mouths
will we let fear silence us

Not by our hearts
will we allow whole peoples
or countries to be deemed evil

Not by our will
and Not in our name

We pledge resistance

We pledge alliance with those
who have come under attack
for voicing opposition to the war
or for their religion or ethnicity

We pledge to make common cause
with the people of the world
to bring about justice,
freedom and peace

Another world is possible
and we pledge to make it real."

JUST PEACEMAKING

Glen Stassen listed ten pieces of advice for the peacemakers in his book, *Just Peacemaking: Ten Practices for Abolishing War* (New York: Pilgrim Press, 1998). They stand by themselves in elegance and eloquence as lessons for each of us.

1. Support nonviolent direct action.

2. Take independent initiatives to reduce threat.

3. Use cooperative conflict resolution.

4. Acknowledge responsibility for conflict and injustice and seek repentance and forgiveness.

5. Advance democracy, human rights, and religious liberty.

6. Foster just and sustainable economic development.

7. Work with emerging cooperative forces in the international system.

8. Strengthen the United Nations and international efforts for cooperation and human rights.

9. Reduce offensive weapons and weapons trade.

10. Encourage grassroots peacemaking groups and voluntary associations.

198 METHODS OF NONVIOLENT ACTION

These methods were compiled by Dr. Gene Sharp and first published in his 1973 book, The Politics of Nonviolent Action, Vol. 2: The Methods of Nonviolent Action. (Boston: Porter Sargent Publishers, 1973). The book outlines each method and gives information about its historical use.

THE METHODS OF NONVIOLENT PROTEST AND PERSUASION

Formal Statements

1. Public Speeches
2. Letters of opposition or support
3. Declarations by organizations and institutions
4. Signed public statements
5. Declarations of indictment and intention
6. Group or mass petitions

Communications with a Wider Audience

7. Slogans, caricatures, and symbols
8. Banners, posters, and displayed communications
9. Leaflets, pamphlets, and books
10. Newspapers and journals
11. Records, radio, and television
12. Skywriting and earthwriting

Group Representations

13. Deputations
14. Mock awards
15. Group lobbying
16. Picketing
17. Mock elections

Symbolic Public Acts

18. Displays of flags and symbolic colors
19. Wearing of symbols

20. Prayer and worship

21. Delivering symbolic objects

22. Protest disrobings

23. Destruction of own property

24. Symbolic lights

25. Displays of portraits

26. Paint as protest

27. New signs and names

28. Symbolic sounds

29. Symbolic reclamations

30. Rude gestures

Pressures on Individuals

31. "Haunting" officials

32. Taunting officials

33. Fraternization

34. Vigils

Drama and Music

35. Humorous skits and pranks

36. Performances of plays and music

37. Singing

Processions

38. Marches

39. Parades

40. Religious processions

41. Pilgrimages

42. Motorcades

Honoring the Dead

43. Political mourning

44. Mock funerals

45. Demonstrative funerals

46. Homage at burial places

Public Assemblies

47. Assemblies of protest or support

48. Protest meetings

49. Camouflaged meetings of protest

50. Teach-ins

Withdrawal and Renunciation

51. Walk-outs

52. Silence

53. Renouncing honors

54. Turning one's back

THE METHODS OF SOCIAL NON-COOPERATION

Ostracism of Persons

55. Social boycott

56. Selective social boycott

57. Lysistratic nonaction

58. Excommunication

59. Interdict

Non-cooperation with Social Events, Customs, and Institutions

    60. Suspension of social and sports activities

    61. Boycott of social affairs

    62. Student strike

    63. Social disobedience

    64. Withdrawal from social institutions

Withdrawal from the Social System

    65. Stay-at-home

    66. Total personal non-cooperation

    67. "Flight" of workers

    68. Sanctuary

    69. Collective disappearance

    70. Protest emigration (hijrat)

THE METHODS OF ECONOMIC NON-COOPERATION: (1) ECONOMIC BOYCOTTS

Actions by Consumers

    71. Consumers' boycott

    72. Nonconsumption of boycotted goods

    73. Policy of austerity

    74. Rent withholding

    75. Refusal to rent

    76. National consumers' boycott

    77. International consumers' boycott

Action by Workers and Producers

78. Workmen's boycott

79. Producers' boycott

Action by Middlemen

80. Suppliers' and handlers' boycott

Action by Owners and Management

81. Traders' boycott

82. Refusal to let or sell property

83. Lockout

84. Refusal of industrial assistance

85. Merchants' "general strike"

Action by Holders of Financial Resources

86. 86. Withdrawal of bank deposits

87. 87. Refusal to pay fees, dues, and assessments

88. 88. Refusal to pay debts or interest

89. 89. Severance of funds and credit

90. 90. Revenue refusal

91. 91. Refusal of a government's money

Action by Governments

92. Domestic embargo

93. Blacklisting of traders

94. International sellers' embargo

111. Working-to-rule strike

112. Reporting "sick" (sick-in)

113. Strike by resignation

114. Limited strike

115. Selective strike

Multi-Industry Strikes

116. Generalized strike

117. General strike

Combination of Strikes and Economic Closures

118. Hartal

119. Economic shutdown

THE METHODS OF POLITICAL NON-COOPERATION

Rejection of Authority

120. Withholding or withdrawal of allegiance

121. Refusal of public support

122. Literature and speeches advocating resistance

Citizens' Noncooperation with Government

123. Boycott of legislative bodies

124. Boycott of elections

125. Boycott of government employment and positions

126. Boycott of government depts., agencies, and other bodies

127. Withdrawal from government educational institutions

128. Boycott of government-supported organizations

129. Refusal of assistance to enforcement agents

130. Removal of own signs and placemarks

131. Refusal to accept appointed officials

132. Refusal to dissolve existing institutions

Citizens' Alternatives to Obedience

133. Reluctant and slow compliance

134. Nonobedience in absence of direct supervision

135. Popular nonobedience

136. Disguised disobedience

137. Refusal of an assemblage or meeting to disperse

138. Sitdown

139. Non-cooperation with conscription and deportation

140. Hiding, escape, and false identities

141. Civil disobedience of "illegitimate" laws

Action by Government Personnel

142. Selective refusal of assistance by government aides

143. Blocking of lines of command and information

144. Stalling and obstruction

145. General administrative non-cooperation

146. Judicial non-cooperation

147. Deliberate inefficiency and selective non-cooperation by enforcement agents

148. Mutiny

Domestic Governmental Action

149. Quasi-legal evasions and delays

150. Non-cooperation by constituent governmental units

International Governmental Action

151. Changes in diplomatic and other representations

152. Delay and cancellation of diplomatic events

153. Withholding of diplomatic recognition

154. Severance of diplomatic relations

155. Withdrawal from international organizations

156. Refusal of membership in international bodies

157. Expulsion from international organizations

THE METHODS OF NONVIOLENT INTERVENTION

Psychological Intervention

158. Self-exposure to the elements

159. The fast

   a) Fast of moral pressure

   b) Hunger strike

   c) Satyagrahic fast

160. Reverse trial

161. Nonviolent harassment

Physical Intervention

162. Sit-in

163. Stand-in

164. Ride-in

165. Wade-in

166. Mill-in

167. Pray-in

168. Nonviolent raids

169. Nonviolent air raids

170. Nonviolent invasion

171. Nonviolent interjection

172. Nonviolent obstruction

173. Nonviolent occupation

Social Intervention

174. Establishing new social patterns

175. Overloading of facilities

176. Stall-in

177. Speak-in

178. Guerrilla theater

179. Alternative social institutions

180. Alternative communication system

Economic Intervention

181. Reverse strike

182. Stay-in strike

183. Nonviolent land seizure

184. Defiance of blockades

185. Politically motivated counterfeiting

186. Preclusive purchasing

187. Seizure of assets

188. Dumping

189. Selective patronage

190. Alternative markets

191. Alternative transportation systems

192. Alternative economic institutions

Political Intervention

193. Overloading of administrative systems

194. Disclosing identities of secret agents

195. Seeking imprisonment

196. Civil disobedience of "neutral" laws

197. Work-on without collaboration

198. Dual sovereignty and parallel government

Source: Gene Sharp, The Politics of Nonviolent Action, Vol. 2: The Methods of Nonviolent Action (Boston: Porter Sargent Publishers, 1973).

"THERE IS NO WAY TO PEACE. PEACE IS THE WAY"

"There is no way to peace. Peace is the Way"

In Deepak Chopra (2005) *Peace is the Way*.
New York: Three Rivers Press.

The **Caritas Path to Peace** is grounded in Caring Science and the deeper Ethic of "BELONGING" and the Ethics of "FACE" (Levinas, 1996) which makes new/old connections between Human Caring and Peace – all related to sustaining humanity at this point in human history. Basic human values of Loving- Kindness, Equanimity, Compassion, Forgiveness and Tolerance, all messages from wisdom teachers, spiritual leaders and sages across time, are embedded in the 'faces' of our global community, and the human caring practices throughout the history and tradition of nursing and other human service professions. These global and universal messages and values also are embedded in extant theories, contemporary science, and philosophies guiding human caring and healing for self, other, our world. Caring Science moves from human caring to eco-caring, proclaiming peaceful relations, honoring all living things.

"… Individual authenticity lies in what we can find that is worth living for. And the only thing worth living for is love. Love of one another. Love for ourselves. Love of our work. Love of our destiny, whatever it may be. Love for our difficulties. Love of life. The love that could free us from the mysterious cycles of suffering. The Love that releases us from our self-imprisonment, from our bitterness, our greed, our madness –engendering competiveness. The love that can make us breathe again. Love a great and beautiful cause, a wonderful vision. A great love for another, or for the future. The love that reconciles us to ourselves, to our simple joys, and to our undiscovered repletion. A creative love. A love touched with the sublime" (Okri, 1997: 56- 57).

Thus, the *Caritas Path of Peace* book invites us into the field of **Infinite Love:** the highest level of *Caritas* Consciousness, uniting humanity across continents, worlds and time, into the constellations of the cosmos of Spirit Divine. *Caritas Path of Peace* provides the basis for intellectual, experiential, philosophical and artistic engagements to sustain human existence and Mother Earth for a great shift of human-kind. Human-to-human, spirit-to-spirit connections, begin with inner peace, radiating out to others, returning us to the heart of peace in the world.

We as health professionals, know, that when we step into the theories and philosophies of human caring, we step into a deep ethic and life practice that connects us with the heart of our humanity, of healing the whole; it is here in this connection, we touch the mystery of inner and outer peace that unites humanity across time and space around the world for a shared soul's journey on the Earth Plane. This expanded worldview raises new questions and offers new connections between personal and planetary transformation related to caring, peace, and the power of Love. Such core perspectives on Caring and Peace introduce caring as an ethical covenant with humanity.

The *Caritas Path to Peace,* Caring Science and *Caritas* Consciousness ask and invite new questions:

- What is Peace?
- What is the origin of peace?
- What is inner peace? How do we obtain it?
- How do we manifest and sustain human caring and peace in our heart, mind, and daily acts?
- Is there a connection between inner peace and outer peace?
- Is the *Caritas Path of Peace* the way to a conscious soul Journey for our human evolution on heaven and on earth?

These foundational yet rhetorical questions can only be addressed from our heart binding philosophical, ethical and practical ideals from the Latin notion of *Caritas* and Caring Science. This focus brings together principles and practices which invite us to consider our common tasks as humans on the Earth plane in order to sustain human dignity, basic civility, and humanity, soul journey in Heaven and on Earth.

As the Peace Path awakens a global Caritas Community, we awaken to walking a shared human –soul journey on earth. These global soul bound tasks for Caritas Peace, include:

- Healing our relationship with Self and Other as the beginning of inner and outer peace; this includes self -acceptance and holding compassion, loving-kindness, forgiveness and tenderness to self, first, thus opening our hearts to accept other with loving kindness and compassion;

- Awakening to Spirit by understanding Human suffering and finding new meanings to live with and transform human suffering, shared as a universal human condition which unites all;

- Finding new depth of meaning in life and all the vicissitudes of the shared human condition of living, change, loss, grief, death, and dying, honoring the enduring human spirit in the midst of impermanence; Awakening to our soul's journey on Earth;

- Finding personal meaning in the life-death cycle and death itself, as part of the larger sacred circle of infinity;

- Coming to terms with our own death and dying – engaging in conscious dying preparations for soul's journey back to Spirit/ mystery;

- "Remembering" – or awakening to the deep nature of life and LOVE; awakening to the "Ethic of Belonging" to infinite field of Universal Love and One world.- that underneath it all, LOVE is all there is that unites and binds human-earth – cosmos existence – holding the Planet together through the Energy of LOVE.

But it is here in this unknown, yet familiar place, the 'still point' in the midst of the dance of life, which this book: the *Caritas Path of Peace*, invites us to enter. For it is here in this space, in this very moment, that we find our way 'home'. Home to our primordial space and Source of our Being and 'Belonging' : A Passage to the heart of our human family: Universal Infinite Love that surrounds, binds and unites one Heart, One Mind, One World- One Cosmos. It is here in this secret space and place that we search inwardly for peace, and there we find the origin of Caring, Compassion, Forgiveness and Tolerance, the basis of Peace: Caritas!

Naming and awakening to the shared human tasks of life itself inform human caring and peaceful actions, which if honored today, can help to save succeeding generations from violence and untold human sorrow, despair and destruction of humanity and Planet Earth itself.

….As Caritas practitioners perhaps we have a new role in the world. To transform the vision of human health and healing by engaging in service to self and society at a different level, by creating 'the energetic field of Caritas', through both overt and subtle practices that transmit and affect the field of the whole. We do this one by one and become part of creating a deeper level of humanity by transforming fundamentally what happens in a given moment, in a given situation, by experimenting with "Being –the-Caritas-Field". This is the truly noble work of nursing and healing that transcends the conventional ego-way of thinking…when we proceed and attain this new old level of Spirit wisdom…in this line of thinking, there is a connection between Caring (as connecting with, sustaining, and deepening our shared humanity) and Peace in the world. In these noble Caritas practices we become Bodhisattvas: those who bless others and who become a blessing to self and others. We actively affect the entire universal field of humanity. (Watson, 2008:48).

As all of us awaken to our gifts and purpose on the earth plane we discover through our *Caritas* Path of Peace Practices, we are contributing to the global evolution of human consciousness and a moral community of caring and peace in our world and perhaps worlds beyond into the Cosmos of Spirit Divine.

I conclude with the World Charter for Human Caring and Peace, developed for beginning the Caritas Path of Peace Pilgrimage in conjunctions with the International Hiroshima Caring and Peace Conference, March, 2012 in Hiroshima, Japan ,co- sponsored by The

Red Cross University ,Hiroshima College of Nursing, Japan and Watson Caring Science Institute, Boulder, Colorado.

Endorsed by American Holistic Nursing Organization, International Association of Human Caring, International Reflective Practice Group, and Healing Touch Education.

INTERNATIONAL CHARTER for HUMAN CARING AND PEACE

by Jean Watson, PhD, RN

TO BE PRESENTED AT THE FIRST ASIAN –PACIFIC INTERNATIONAL CARITAS CONSORTIUM AND INTERNATIONAL CARING AND PEACE CONFERENCE: HIROSHIMA, JAPAN, MARCH , 2012.

PROLOGUE AND BASIC PREMISES:

At this time in human history the survival of humanity and Earth Mother's eco-system is threatened. Every human on earth shares and draws upon Earth Mother/Sky Father and helps to evolve the Planet with caring for all. Each society sustains human caring and humanity for the whole. The practices of human caring are practices of peace.

In order to sustain humanity and the Planet Earth, the following premises are proclaimed as a formal Charter for Human Caring and Peace:

- Every human on earth has a right to be treated with respect and dignity;
- Every person in the world has the right to receive humane and compassionate care;
- Every human on earth shares and draws upon all the ecosystem for survival;;
- Every human is here on the earth plane for a reason and unique life- purpose;
- All of humanity is joined in the infinite field of the universe with each other and all living things; All creation is sacred and connected;

- Each person's level of humanity reflects upon the whole, allowing for the collective growth of human consciousness for all of humankind;
- Globally, women and children carry the predominance of human caring for all of humanity, helping to sustain human caring and humanity for the whole;
- The human caring needs of women and children in the world are threatened;
- All humans are entitled to be free of tyranny, violation, abuse – free to pursue their dreams and follow their heart;
- All humans 'Belong' to Infinite Source, the sacred mystery, which unites ALL, before, during and after the Planet Earth plane experience.
- Finally, if we want to sustain human caring and peace, begin first with personal self -caring and private and public practices of inner Peace.   If we practice caring and inner/outer peace with self, others, and our Planet Earth we are contributing to Peace in our world, through our individual and collective roles and actions.

Therefore, ON BEHALF OF THESE BASIC HUMAN CARING VALUES AND PREMISES, which sustain human caring and contribute to peace in our world, WATSON CARING SCIENCE INSTITUTE INTRODUCES THE INTERNATIONAL CHARTER FOR HUMAN CARING AND PEACE.

Jean Watson

KEY REFERENCES:

Samuels, Michael; Lane, Mary, (1999) Creative Healing, San Francisco, Harper

Samuels, Michael; Lane, Mary, (2000) Spirit Body Healing, New York, Wiley

Samuels, Michael; Lane, Mary, (2000) Path of the Feather, New York, Putnam

Samuels, Michael; Lane, Mary, (2002) Shaman Wisdom, New York, Wiley.

Chopra, Deepak. (2005) *Peace is the Way.* New York: Three Rivers Press.

Levinas, E. (1996) *Totality & Infinity.* Pittsburgh: Duquesne University Press.

Okri, B. (1997). *A Way of Being Free.* London: Phoenix.

Watson, J. (2006) *Caring Science as Sacred Science.* Philadelphia: FA Davis.

Watson, J. (2008) *Nursing. The Philosophy and Science of Caring.* Boulder, CO.: University Press of Colorado.

Watson, J. (2012). Human Caring Science. Sudbury, Massachusetts: Jones & Bartlett.

Watson, J. International Charter for Human Caring and Peace. May 2011.

www.HeartMath.com;

www.HeartMath.org

www.watsoncaringscience.org

ABOUT THE AUTHORS.

Mary Rockwood Lane, R.N., Ph.D. FAAN., is a professor, nurse and painter. She is the co-founder of the *Arts in Medicine program* at University of Florida, Gainesville and founded their artist in residence program. She developed and led that program for over ten years. She is Assistant Professor of Nursing at University of Florida College of Nursing where she teaches Creativity and Spirituality in Healthcare. She has written many articles on creativity and healthcare in nursing and medical journals and is a recognized leader in the field. She lectures and teaches workshops on creativity and spirituality in healthcare across the world and helps medical centers and artists set up art and healing programs. Dr. Lane did peer reviewed research on how the spirit heals at University of Florida for her PhD.

Her interest in peace came from her family and childhood. Her father was a career military, a Lt. Colonial in Air Force intelligence in Turkey. In WWII he was one of the soldiers who liberated the concentration camps and told Mary this story when she was a child. Her brother Capt. Larry Rockwood was a career military officer and was arrested attempting to free Haitian political prisoners. He is considered a hero and model of ethical military action; he followed his heart, not orders, and was court marshaled for his peaceful social action.

She is co-author with Michael Samuels of *Creative Healing, Spirit-Body Healing, The Path of the Feather*, and *Shaman Wisdom, Shaman Healing*. She is Associate Professor of Nursing at University of Florida College of Nursing where she teaches Spirituality and Creativity in Nursing.

Mary Rockwood Lane works with Jean Watson as a trainer in the Caritas technique and is on the board of Directors of Watson Caring Science Institute. She will present at the Conference for Peace in Hiroshima, 2011.

Michael Samuels, M.D. has used guided imagery for spiritual visions with cancer patients for over twenty five years in private practice and in consultation. He teaches Art in Healing at San Francisco State

Institute of holistic Studies and at JFK graduate school of arts and consciousness. He was on the advisory boards of Commonweal, for their Cancer Retreats, and Tamalpa Institute for healing dance. He is also the founder and director of *Art As a Healing Force*, a project started in 1990 devoted to making art and healing. He lectures and does workshops nationwide for physicians, nurses, artists, and patients on healing. He has organized many nationwide conferences on healing and visits and participates in projects in hospitals where art and music are used with patients.

His interest in peace started when he attended Friends Academy Locust Valley N.Y. for high school. There he was immersed in pacifist Quaker teachings, and attended meeting each week as he grew up. During the Viet Nam war, he was physician on the Hopi and Navaho Reservation as alternative service as a Conscientious Objector.

He is the author of eighteen books including the best selling *Well Body Book*, *Well Baby Book*, *Well Pregnancy Book*, and the imagery classic, *Seeing With the Mind's Eye*. He is the co-author with Mary Rockwood Lane of *Creative Healing, How Art, Writing, Dance and Music Can Heal Body and Soul, Spirit-Body Healing: Using Your Mind's Eye to Unlock the Medicine Within*, and *The Path of the Feather: A Handbook and kit for Making Medicine Wheels and Meeting Spirit Animals, Shaman Wisdom, Shaman Healing, How to Use Visionary and Spiritual tools to heal* . He lives in Tinos, Greece and Bolinas, California and has two grown sons.

My life work has been about the following, in one way or another: Asking and reflecting for myself and others:

How do I/we walk through life?

How do I/we get our footing to bring human caring, love, and healing, for our self and all other living beings?

What is the path that awakens us to the heart of our shared humanity?

Our connection with Mother Earth? Our oneness with Source – the infinite unitary field of cosmic loving consciousness?

How do I/we navigate our personal journey toward higher deeper evolution of consciousness of Human Caring? How do we wake up to realize: Caring itself is THE PATH for inner and outer Peace?

Often unbeknownst to them and society alike, nurses are the silent peacemakers on the earth. They offer profound gifts, sustaining humane caring through daily, simple, yet profound acts of caring, compassion, and love. They offer themselves to serve that which is greater than self, to sustain both human and planetary survival.

My life work has been a covenant with our shared humanity - a walking, writing, talking, teaching, living pilgrimage, literally and metaphorically, offering deep spirit filled, soul messages about the depth, magnitude and magnificence of our humanity; informing and inviting others to see and experience self-caring: the beauty, truth, compassion, and connections in themselves and all our relations.   This path is an inward path, to awakened to inner space from which radiates heart-centered loving, caring, peaceful acts and actions in our world. Along my journey, I tired of my own talking, so I engaged in a personal silent pilgrimage to 'energetically' and literally walk my words and my heart longing for humanity's healing, into the Earth herself. It was a pilgrimage for my own caring and healing, taken in 2005: El Camino (the Way) to Santiago de Compostela, Northern Spain (Watson, J. 2006) Walking pilgrimage as Caritas Action in the world. Journal of Holistic Nursing. 24(4):289-296).

Walking pilgrimage, whether at home or open field, serves as a metaphor for discovering our sacred path for this earth's journey.

The Caritas Path of Peace book is a culmination of my life's work, serving as a vehicle for the continuation of my pilgrimage around the globe as a global invitation to nurses and others to join us on this walk, imprinting our caring peaceful conscious connections into the earthly realm of our everyday life. If just one nurse, one person begins the spiritual pilgrimage toward Caritas connections for peace, we all will be closer to our Source - elevating the consciousness of the planet toward healing and Divine love.

May this work serve as a touchstone to help us all pay attention to the steps and footprints we make along the way of our life journey. I invite you - yes, YOU, whomever and wherever you are, to walk this Caritas Path of Peace with us and millions of nurses around the earth's orbit.

Made in the USA
Lexington, KY
13 October 2014